# The Redneck Guide to Raisin' Children

# The Redneck Guide to Raisin' Children

Annie and Glen-Bob Smith

Illustrations by Dick Kulpa

St. Martin's Griffin ⚐ New York

Design by Ellen R. Sasahara

Library of Congress Cataloging-in-Publication Data

Smith, Annie.
    The redneck guide to raisin' children / Annie and Glen-Bob Smith.
—1st ed.
        p.    cm.
    ISBN 0-312-18163-9
    1. Rednecks—Humor.    2. Child rearing—Humor.    3. Parenting—
Humor.    I. Smith, Glen-Bob.    II. Title.
    PN6231.R38S65    1998
    818'.5407—dc21                                               97-40967

First St. Martin's Griffin Edition: January 1998

10  9  8  7  6  5  4  3  2  1

Books are available in quantity for promotional or premium use. Write to Director of Special Sales, St. Martin's Press, 175 Fifth Avenue, New York, NY 10010, for information on discounts and terms, or call toll-free (800) 221-7945. In New York, call (212) 674-5151 (ext. 645).

# Contents

Why We Wrote This Book    ix

All about Conceiving Your Child    1

Hauling Your Newborn Home    1
Recording the Birth    2
Fixing Up the Nursery    2

Breast-Feeding Directions    5

Bottle Feeding    5
Weaning the Baby    6

Changing Rug Rats' Diapers    7

Choosing a Baby-sitter    7
Redneck Nannies    8
"Whut Air Ya Gonna Name the Kid?"    9
Middle Names    10
Hollywood in the Backwoods    10
The Significance of *Bubba*    12
Dolls' Real Purpose    13

Dating outside the Family    15

Explaining Eviction to Your Kids    17

# Contents

Farting: Will You Go to Hell?    19

Passing Gas for Fun and Profit    21

Grime and Punishment    23

When Grandpa's in Prison    24
Just Say "Hell, No!" to Drugs    25
Stranger in a Strange Land    27
Surefire Cussin' Remedies    28

Huntin' and Fishin'    29

When Nature Calls Collect    30
Guns and Gun Racks    30

In-laws and Other Household Pests    32

Debugging Your Home    33

Junkyards as Vacation Sites    34

Other Family Outings    36

Keeping Your Kids Safe    39

Lip-Smackin' Snacks for Kids    42

The Real Dirt on Eatin' Right    43
This Is Your Brain on Fried Eggs    44
Outside Dinin'    46

Moonshine and Other Medications    47

Home First Aid for Kids    48
Stuttering    49

Nine Greatest Redneck Tragedies    50

Outhouse Dos and Don'ts    53

Entertaining in the Outhouse    54

# Contents

## Putting the X Back in Christmas    57

The Redneck Stock Portfolio    58
Hardheaded Hillbillies in a Software World    58

## Quaint Redneck Superstitions    61

Elvis: Dead or Alive?    62
Bedtime Stories and Lullabies    63

## Redneck Toys    65

All Their Rowdy Friends    67
Sixteen Uses for an Old Commode    68
A Boy's First Truck    71
A Boy's First DUI    73

## School Days, Rule Days    74

The Birds, the Bees, and the Backseat    76
Sex, Lies, and Duck Tape    77

## Twins: Should You Keep Just One?    79

## Use and Care of Snot Rags    81

## Vaseline's Role in Rearin'    82

Sideburns for Young'uns under Ten    82
More Grooming Tips    83
The Little Redneck Instruction Book    83

## Weighing Kids on Store Scales    85

Child Rearing for Peanuts    85
The Britches of Mayhew County    87
Night of the Living T-shirt    88
Buying Brand-New Duds    90
Manners    90
Courtesy    91

# Contents

**X Marks the Pot**   93

Redneck Home Furnishings   93

**Young'uns Gotta Work**   96

The Man with the Goal 'n' Gun   96
Callus Behavior   97
Picking the Right Job   98
Shorty's Rise to Riches   99
Dumb and Dumber   102

**Zero Tolerance for Misbehavin'**   103

Passing Out Chores   104
Passing Out in Front of the Kids   104
The Boogeyman: Parents' Best Friend   105
The Haunted Pillow Caper   106
Give 'Em That Old-Time Religion   106
Picking the Right Church   107
Give Us This Day Our Daily Cornbread   108
Skinny-dipping during Baptism   109
Speaking in Unknown Tongues   109
Say Hello to Hell   110
Honky-tonk Survival Skills   110
Entering the Outside World   112
How to Act like a Redneck   113
Beer: It's Not Just for Breakfast Anymore   116
How to Beat Procrastination   116

# Why We Wrote This Book

We've raised ten kids and not a single one of 'em has gone to prison. So we reckon that makes us qualified to tell other people how to bring up their young'uns.

Our five grown boys all hold down good jobs making over six dollars an hour. Our three married daughters also work outside the home, hanging clothes on the line and mowing the yard. The two youngest kids, Lonnie and Betty Jean, still live with us. They're more rambunctious than their older brothers and sisters, but we blame that on the TV. No matter—we expect them to turn out well or else we'll tan their hides.

Now, we don't claim to be some highfalutin experts on child rearing like that baby-care fellow Mr. Spock. We're just raising our young'uns like our own parents brought us up, and we're passing along these time-tested methods to you.

Most redneck boys and girls are polite, law-abiding kids who make their parents proud. The worst four-letter words they use are "shucks" and "dadburn." And it ain't no accident that they turned out decent.

It's because they got raised the right way—the redneck way.

That's our way, and it works. We know because we're parents, and neither one of us has ended up in the crazy house yet.

Annie and Glen-Bob Smith
Rural Route 8
Chicken Neck, Tennessee
555–2218 (Our neighbor's phone—ask him to holler for us.)

# All about Conceiving Your Child

If you don't know how to do this, you ain't ready to care for the result.

## Hauling Your Newborn Home

Steal a blanket from the hospital—heck, they're gonna over-charge you anyway—and wrap it around your baby so he'll keep warm during the ride home.

This is especially important if it's wintertime and your pickup truck's heater is broke. You might be used to flicking icicles off your chin on the way to work, but the baby just came from a nice warm belly and will squall all the way home if he's cold.

If the blanket has the hospital's name on it, so much the better. In some Southern neighborhoods that's like having de-signer label bedsheets. Rednecks love "name brand" furnishings in their homes—that's why they hang Budweiser mirrors on their den walls and permanently borrow Budget Inn ashtrays.

In fact, when you take that blanket, see if you also can pocket a saucer with the hospital's name on it. Put it beside the baby's bed so he can use it for an ashtray when he starts sneaking smokes six or seven years down the road.

Once the kid was outgrowed the blanket, put it away. Give

it back when he gets old enough to drive. It'll be a fond reminder of his childhood.

He can also tear it in two and use half as a gas cap and the other half as a snot rag.

# Recording the Birth

Unlike certain beers, kids don't come with a "Born On" date. So as soon as you get home from the hospital, write down your baby's birthday in the family Bible. That way you won't forget it—which is easy to do if you've got a houseful of young'uns.

There ain't nothing more embarrassing than showing off your latest child to a neighbor and having to say, "This is our daughter Sally. She was born last year, some'ers between the time the dog died and the roof fell in."

# Fixing Up the Nursery

Clear a space out in the backyard. Be sure to pick up all the busted beer bottles, shotgun shell casings, and any other trash your kids might get cut or choked on.

But don't move all of the old commodes. Leave the cleanest, least cracked one in the nursery area. Toilet training's a messy job, so make the kids learn it for themselves.

Next, put up four posts and string some chicken wire around the nursery. Make sure the fence ain't got no holes in it. You don't want your babies crawling around the neighborhood—a dirty-faced kid looks very much like a raccoon and some fool might take a potshot at it.

When it rains, don't bother bringing your young'uns inside unless it's a real frog drowner. A good drizzle on Saturday means you won't have to bother giving the kids their weekly bath, and you'll have time to watch all of *Walker, Texas Ranger*.

Meet Maw Redneck

# Breast-Feeding Directions

Rednecks traditionally have big families, and redneck women traditionally have big bosoms. We've got women in our hometown of Chicken Neck, Tennessee, who make Dolly Parton look like she's got two ball bearings taped to her chest.

But no matter if you're a 44DDD, the rule is still: One Baby Per Breast!

We don't see anything wrong with breast-feeding your babies in public. But a woman trying to fit three or four babies on two nipples looks kinda like a hog suckling piglets. It's downright upsetting to genteel folk.

Even worse, the babies who don't get enough milk will grow up conniving and mean. We think this is what causes lawyers and politicians.

## Bottle Feeding

A few unlucky women, God bless 'em, have breasts the size of acorns. Or even if they do have decent-sized bosoms, they don't have much milk. In these cases it's okay for them to raise their kids on baby formula.

But you have to buy the right formula. For instance, Formula 409 won't do—although it'll sure give your young'uns the cleanest innards around.

Shorty Perkins, who owns one-eighth interest in the local filling station, accidentally bought his kid some Formula One racing fuel additive. It tasted terrible, but for a while there his little boy Scooter was the fastest kid in Mayhew County.

## Weaning the Baby

Sooner or later, mothers have to uncouple their young'uns from their bosom.

If the kid keeps hanging on until it weighs upwards of fifty pounds, Mama's stretched breasts are going to take aim directly at her feet the rest of her life.

If you reach that point, even the Wonderbra saleswoman can't help. She'll just throw up her hands and send you to a body shop that custom-makes bras with steel-belted radial supports.

So get that young'un's mouth off your bosom as soon as you can. If he won't let go, run down to the volunteer fire department and have them pry him loose with the Jaws of Life. The next step is to put something else into your child's hungry little mouth.

Jars of baby food work fine. Mashed peas, pinto beans, and okra are popular in the redneck world. Finely ground hog jowls also will do, but they might upset a baby's delicate stomach.

We've found that most babies love cold milk with hot cornbread crumbled up in it—which is easy to eat when you ain't got all your teeth.

Maybe that's why rednecks of all ages love cornbread and milk.

# Changing Rug Rats' Diapers

This is a dirty, thankless chore. That's why lots of redneck parents let their small tots run around naked from the waist down and let the chips fall where they may.

Keep your little'uns out in the nursery most of the time and eventually they'll set aside one corner to use as an outhouse. Then you can just go out with a pooper scooper and clean up once a day. This saves on diaper costs and diapering time.

You don't even have to buy diapers when company's coming. Just pin a dishcloth or snot rag over your baby's bottom and hope for the best.

## Choosing a Baby-sitter

Go down to the pawn shop and pick out a good cheap VCR (the best ones have "12:00" flashing on the front). Then find a tape of *Smokey and the Bandit*—which is probably the best movie ever made.

You can sneak out of the house for hours while your kids are busy watching and rewatching that wonderful Burt Reynolds movie, which somehow was overlooked at Oscar time.

Last summer our neighbor Rufus McKinney put out a pile of Little Debbie cakes, turned on *Smokey*, and took his missus to Myrtle Beach—and their young'uns didn't realize they were gone until three days later when a storm knocked out the power.

Some rednecks use the regular TV to baby-sit their kids, but it's not as good as *Smokey* and the VCR. The quality of network TV has gone straight downhill ever since they took *The Gong Show* off the air.

## Rednecks' Five Favorite Videos

1. *Smokey and the Bandit*

2. *Smokey and the Bandit II*

3. *Smokey and the Bandit III*

4. *The Alamo (John Wayne version)*

5. *The Beverly Hillbillies: The Movie*

## Redneck Nannies

In good weather, make your littlest kids play outside in the yard. Tie a nanny goat nearby and warn the young'uns that if they're mean, the nanny will butt 'em on the butt. Tell the kids: "If your nanny says '*bah-ah-ah-ah,*' you'd better straighten up fast— or you'll have to *stand* up for the next week!"

Once the young'uns are grown, you can eat the goat and mount its head on your den wall.

## "Whut Air Ya Gonna Name the Kid?"

You'll hear this question from everybody you know as soon as word gets around town that you've added to your litter.

A lot of your friends will even hint for you to name your latest young'un after them, even though you're pretty sure they're not the father or mother.

It's real vital to pick the right name because, as sure as the sun will rise tomorrow, the wrong name will scar a boy or girl for life. Listen to Johnny Cash's song "A Boy Named Sue" and you'll see what we're talking about.

We used to know a boy whose parents named him Leslie, after Leslie Howard in *Gone with the Wind*, and the kid spent years trying to overcome that sissy name.

When he reached his teen years, he became a rebel and tried his best to look tough and act mean.

He sent off a letter asking to join the Hell's Angels biker gang. Only problem was, the kid kinda fit his name—he was a bit, well, prissy—and the screening committee appointed by the Hell's Angels CEO rejected Leslie's application "with deepest regrets."

Leslie went ahead with his biker plans anyway, on his own. He got a mean-looking dagger tattooed on his left forearm, with a banner wrapped around it that said Born to Raise Gerbils.

He bought an old '64 Harley-Davidson from Shorty Perkins. But Leslie had to take a door-to-door sales job to pay for the bike, and he looked kind of ridiculous roaring around town on his big hog with a little pink bumper sticker that said Ask Me about Mary Kay Cosmetics.

Leslie finally gave up fighting his name and moved to San Francisco. Last we heard, he owned a styling salon.

It broke his truck-driver daddy Sam's heart.

9

Sam had always dreamed of owning a styling salon.

So if you want to avoid heartache for yourself and your kids, *don't* slap a girlie-sounding name on your baby boy—or a boy-sounding name on your girl.

And shy away from giving your young'uns highfalutin names. A fancy moniker like Granville, Heathcliff, or Regan will get the kid laughed out of grade school. Even the teachers will have to stifle a snicker when they call the roll.

Besides, your kid probably won't be able to spell his own name until he's old enough to buy beer.

## Middle Names

Many rednecks use their middle names as part of their first names—such as Roy Lee, Glen-Bob, or Sammi Jo. So pick a middle name your child will be proud to use.

Professor Harland K. Sampson has a good example of a bad middle name. For years the little perfessor told everybody the *K* stood for *Kounty*—as in Harlan County, Kentucky—but then we found out his middle name actually was Konan.

Professor Sampson's a shy, quiet bookworm. So once the truth came out, naturally his students nicknamed him Konan the Librarian.

## Hollywood in the Backwoods

N*ever* name your boy or girl after a movie star, unless it's Burt, Sally, or Chuck. Star names might look wonderful and glamorous on a birth certificate, but you have to remember that the young'un will be stuck with the name for life.

Don't you think it's downright strange that five of today's

top movie tough guys are named Sylvester, Arnold, Steven, Bruce, and Jean-Claude? With snicker-sparking names like that, no wonder they go around shooting people!

Instead, do like most redneck parents do: Pass along the same names from generation to generation to generation, *ad inflamation*.

Traditional country boys' names usually end in a *y*—such as Billy, Andy, Tommy, or Jimmy.

And a popular way to end girls' names is with an *e*—such as Pauline, Annie, Charlene, or Aldie. But forget Goldie and Sophie.

If you want to get a little highfalutin, part the kid's first and middle names with a hyphen.

One of our longtime family favorites is Glen-Bob. Feel free to use it as many times as you like, at no charge.

But since the name belongs to the Smith clan, make sure your boy always writes it this way: Glen-Bob®.

Some people name their kids after towns. We've heard of little girls called Chamonix (France), Athens (Tennessee), and Tiffany (New York). We believe this practice can get risky.

What if some parents in our town named their little girl Chicken Neck?

As we all know, Sylvester Stallone's famous boxer, Rocky, was named after the Rocky Mountains. But most parents don't want their kids dragging a place's name around behind them all through life.

When Rufus McKinney's wife birthed their last daughter, the transplanted Yankee doctor who delivered her asked: "Have you chosen an appellation?" Rufus told him he wasn't about to name his kid after a mountain.

## Rednecks' Five Favorite Names for Girls

1. Audrey

2. Annie

3. Earlene

4. Josie Mae

5. Polly

## Rednecks' Five Favorite Names for Boys

1. Ray

2. Earl

3. Bobby

4. Walter

5. Sammy

# The Significance of *Bubba*

After redneck parents pick a formal name for their child, they always end up calling him or her by a nickname. But you've gotta be careful about that, too.

For example, don't nickname a little boy Bubba. In the South,

Bubba is almost like a royal title bestowed on deserving people.

A boy's got to earn that name through heroic actions like carrying an old lady's refrigerator across the street or shooting up a jukebox.

And anybody named Bubba has got to be BIG.

Alan Autry—who plays hard-muscled, soft-hearted Sgt. Bubba Skinner on *In the Heat of the Night*—never would be allowed to use that name if he was playing a pencil-thin conniving cop. Outraged rednecks would picket the Sparta courthouse!

Don't nickname a boy Shorty either, unless you're pretty sure he'll never grow taller than three and a half feet.

And don't jokingly slap Shorty on a kid because his zipper is longer than his private part. The boy will turn bitter and grow up to be a criminal or President.

Shorty Perkins doesn't mind being called Shorty because he's really six feet tall. But we reckon he wouldn't be happy today if he'd been nicknamed Skinny because that name fits. He weighs only about 115 pounds soaking wet with a 10-pound security chain on his wallet.

We've seen our kids draw stick figures that looked fatter than Shorty Perkins. Better-lookin', too.

## Dolls' Real Purpose

Most young parents think dolls are things to play with. But in redneck households, they're used mainly to teach little girls how to take care of their own kids one of these days.

Every girl should have six or more dolls. And you should make her wash, burp, dress, and fix meals for them on the hour—all through the night.

Don't buy your kids any fancy porcelain dolls. Get plastic or rag dolls such as Raggedy Anns so they can practice paddling without worrying about breaking the dolls.

What this world needs is dolls that do what real kids do. It would be great if you could give your girl a half dozen dolls that cry, scream, hold their breath, demand candy, sneak cigarettes, and slip out of the house at night to meet dolls of the opposite sex.

There ought to be "Baby Smart Mouth" dolls that contradict everything you say.

And somebody ought to put out a "Baby Chore Helper" doll. When you pull the string, the doll won't even lift a finger—then she'll run out the door as soon as your back is turned.

Until these hit the market, your kids will have to make do with regular store-bought dolls. Or they can make their own dolls out of cornstalks.

To do this, cut a thick four-inch-long piece of stalk for the body. Cut a thinner one-inch piece for the head. Then slice off five slivers of the stalk's hard shell and use them to make the doll's neck, arms, and legs. Next, stick on half-inch sections of stalk for the hands and feet.

Young'uns can even use cornstalks to make a pet dog or cat for their doll.

# Dating outside the Family

Contrary to popular belief, most rednecks *don't* marry close relatives.

Why, half the couples we know ain't related by blood in any way.

Inbreeding leads to all kinds of problems. It can cause retarded kids, and a serious case of lead poisoning if your wife's backwoods family doesn't get along with you.

It can also cause some people to lose all common sense and vote Republican, according to a 1989 study by Professor Harland K. Sampson.[1]

And there's one other problem: In some Southern states, even if you get divorced, you're still legally brother and sister. Which means you're still stuck with seeing your dratted husband or wife once a year at family reunions.

So when your kids get old enough to date, sneak a sample of blood from each teenager and his or her date. It won't be that hard to get blood; redneck kids play so rough, they're always cutting themselves on something.

If the dating couple have the same blood type, odds are

---

1. Professor Harland Konan Sampson, "GOP Ballot Strategies in Chicken Neck," *The Mayhew County Weekly Record* (June 11, 1990): 3. Reprinted without the author's permission or knowledge.

they're related—and it's your beholden duty to squash that budding romance by any means necessary.

If the blood types are different, give them your blessing. But don't let them have that big, lavish shotgun wedding until they both turn sixteen.

# Explaining Eviction
# to Your Kids

Rednecks are not just a mobile-home society, they're a mobile society.

It seems like the landlord comes around pestering redneck tenants for the rent every five or six months, so they have to regularly pack up and move in the middle of the night.

We've got relatives who've moved so often, they keep their outhouse on wheels.

Uncle Billy has lived in fifty-four different houses since fighting in Korea, and he hasn't paid a penny in rent all these years. Landlords won't even come within shouting distance of Billy's home because he's got a steel plate in his head, keeps his old combat carbine beside the front door, and riles easier than a pit bull.

The property owners usually get rid of Billy just like they do a lot of uncooperative renters: They go to court and get eviction papers.

When the sheriff's deputy comes to your door and orders you to get out, here are some explanations you can give your young'uns:

- "Sorry, kids, we have to move. Elvis wants to hide out here for a while."

- "The hound dog snatched the rent money off the table and hid it someplace. You kids seen him digging in the yard?"

• "We just found out our neighbors are aliens and they're going to beam you up to Pluto. There ain't no Burger Kings on Pluto, kids!"

• "Professor Sampson over at the junior college wants to use our family for a double-blind study. Now, we know you kids don't want to spend six weeks wearing dark glasses and carrying white canes."

• "The feds are putting us in the Witness Protection Program because your daddy told on the men at work who kicked the vending machine to get free Pepsis."

# Farting: Will You Go to Hell?

Passing gas is common among rednecks because of the foods they eat. Expect your kids to start doing it early and often, especially if you feed 'em lots of beans.

Professor Harland K. Sampson says his research shows the five biggest causes of natural gas explosions in humans are: (1) pinto beans, (2) October beans, (3) navy beans, (4) cabbage, and (5) anything served at Shoney's.

The worst, of course, are pinto beans. They give you so much gas you could open your own filling station.

Farting is politely called "pooting" in parts of the South, probably because it's a nicer-sounding term than the "F" word.

Although passing gas in public ain't as frowned upon among rednecks as it is among certain other groups, you still should teach your kids when it's sinful. Tell your children:

- *Don't* let a big fart in church. And if you do, don't fix your mother with an accusing look and say real loud, "Well, Mommy!"

- *Don't* poot in school, unless the whole class is doing it and you can't get singled out as the villain.

- *Don't* pass gas at the dinner table. If you feel the urge, run outside and let 'er rip where the breeze can whisk the smell away.

**Redneck drive-by**

When Annie serves soup beans, onions, and cornbread for supper at our house, sometimes the kitchen
table is plumb abandoned. We're all out in the yard, just
a-blowin' in the wind.

One night Rufus McKinney heard our loud poots and
figured we was shooting off firecrackers. He ran outside and
raised his American flag, thinking it was the Fourth of July.

• *Don't* fart in a truck or car when all the windows are rolled up. If you've just got to ease out some gas to relieve belly pains, crack your window first.

Somebody probably will notice the foul smell anyway, so be prepared to say, "Whee-ooo! Must be a lot o' dead rats over at the dump this time o' year!"

Don't worry about people on the street smelling the stink coming out of your car. Redneck pedestrians are used to drive-by pootings.

# Passing Gas for Fun and Profit

Tell your kids it's all right to fart on a date if they do it discreetly, or if they don't really like their companion and never want to see him or her again.

Passing gas also is perfectly acceptable once your young'uns grow up and go out socializing with buddies.

After a few Buds at the bar, some rednecks even have contests to see who can fart the loudest—and the winner gets free beer the rest of the night.

Farting is such a tradition among rednecks that Glen-Bob's daddy even wrote a poem about it. Here are his actual words:

> *How well I know—and you know, too—*
> *Just what a stinking fart can do.*
> *You've got two choices—to hold your breath*
> *Or breathe in and be gassed to death.*
> *I've let 'em myself; they smelt like a dead rat.*
> *I couldn't stand to be where I was at.*
> *You take this polluted air, where did it start?*
> *It started from people letting soup bean farts.*

Our whole family is proud of that poem. We figure Henry Fartsworse Longsmeller couldn't have said it better.

Heed this warning, parents: If your young'uns don't pass a little gas every now and then, they could blow up like a balloon and bust wide open.

So don't let anyone tell your kids that passing gas is wrong, or that it means they're not refined and cultured.

We're sure Miss Manners would turn up her nose at this advice. But if she wasn't constantly turning off people with her snooty rules, she'd be *Mrs.* Manners, wouldn't she?

# Grime and Punishment

When our son Wimpy once borrowed a neighbor boy's bike without asking permission, we punished him by making him cut that family's grass all summer with a push mower.

Some people thought that was a little harsh for Wimpy's first offense.

But Aunt Alma—who, God bless her, sometimes gets her thoughts tongue-tied—sided with us. She said, "He knows which side his bread is buttered on, and now he must lie in it."

So we stuck to our punishment. And guess what? After that sweaty, terrible summer, Wimpy never again ventured into the dark underbelly of the criminal world.

The point of this here story is simple: When your kids cross the line, make the consequences hit 'em as hard as a Mack truck. A slap on the wrist ain't going to keep any young'un straight, but a trip to the woodshed sure might make him think twice the next time.

However, don't be too cruel when you physically punish your young'uns. Our saying is: Children should be seen and not hurt.

Also, teach your kids to respect the law. If it wasn't for deputies, police, and game wardens putting their lives on the line every day, not a single human being or deer would be safe anywhere in the USA.

These brave men and women deserve to be called "sir" by kids. Drill that into your offspring until they do it automatically.

If they don't, they could head down the wrong path and their high school yearbook pictures might have front and side views, with their height clearly marked on the white background.

# When Grandpa's in Prison

Garth Brooks' song saying "Mama's in the graveyard, papa's in the pen," always brings a tear to our eyes when they play it on the radio. That's because it's so true in our household.

Glen-Bob's mama, Mae, passed away six years ago. And his daddy (who asked not to be identified) is serving a year and a half in the state penitentiary.

But unlike Garth's tune, our two tragedies ain't connected.

Poor Mama got whacked by a runaway cotton candy wagon during a visit to Five Flags over Alabama. She was so flattened we had to bury her in a big Domino's pizza box.

Then a second catastrophe hit our family when Daddy got put in the slammer after a run-in with a neighbor.

This low-down drunk was beating his wife and she ran over to Daddy's house to get away. Her husband tried to go in the door after her, so Daddy—who's pushing seventy, but still has his bricklayer muscles—laid the fool out cold.

Daddy always taught us: "Any man who hits a woman ain't much of a man." And he proved it that night, because he purt-near killed the wife beater with just one punch.

So Daddy went to prison for "excessive use of force." And we got stuck with the job of explaining his incarceration to his grandkids and great-grandkids.

This is a ticklish situation. It's embarrassing when you've got a relative in prison, and unfortunately this happens now and then among redneck families.

How do you help your kids cope when Grandpa's in prison?

Here are some ideas we came up with:

1. Hide the awful truth—turn Grandpa into a hero. Tell your children he went looking for the real killer of JFK and mysteriously disappeared from the Texas Book Suppository.

2. Say that Grandpa got a job out of town at a license plate factory, but he'll be back as soon as they get up to *z*.

3. Tell your kids the truth, that Grandpa's behind bars. Then stretch the truth a bit by swearing he was framed—and you're looking for the one-armed man that really done it.

4. Pretend Grandpa's still with you. Set a plate for him at the table. On his birthday, buy a cake and join the grandkids in singing, "For He's a Jolly Good Felon."

5. Make up bumper stickers for your kids' lunch boxes that say PROUD GRANDSON OF A TRUSTEE AT _____ STATE PRISON.

## Just Say "Hell, No!" to Drugs

Drugs are ruining America. Look at all the crime and violence in the big cities. You and your kids ain't safe on some big-city streets unless you're all wearing Middle Ages armor and carrying a four-shot howitzer.

We agree with ol' Charlie Daniels when he sings about taking drug dealers out in the swamp, tying them to a stump, and letting the alligators and snakes do the rest. Crack pushers, especially, are killers and don't deserve to live among us decent folk.

Even Professor Harland K. Sampson, who's as mild-mannered

as Wally Cox, gets hopping mad when he talks about drug dealers. He says they ought to be put on the "endangered feces list."

But sad to say, these lowlifes are always going to be around and tempting your children. So you've got to educate your kids early in life about the dangers of crack, PCP, heroin, and other drugs.

Pound it into your boys that if they get hooked on hard drugs, they'll never be able to afford a pickup truck. That should be enough to scare the wits out of true redneck boys and steer them clear of brain-altering substances.

As for your girls—warn them until you're blue in the face that if they don't resist the lure of drugs, they'll never have a home with a nice new vinyl kitchen floor and genuine Kenmore appliances.

Explain to your children all the good things that come with a drug-free life. For example, they won't have to worry about being rushed by ambulance from the carnival to the hospital . . . they'll never wake up in scary places with even scarier bedmates . . . they won't have to run from some drug-crazed freak . . . and they'll always have a job as long as Wal-Mart and Dunkin' Donuts are in business.

Sadly, despite all the good work being done by Chuck Norris and his "Kick Drugs Out of America" campaign, we'll never completely stop people from using drugs.

Even rednecks get hooked on drugs every now and then. One of the most damaging is uncoated aspirin, which leaves a lot of long-distance truckers with gruesome stomach pains.

We've also known some people who were hopeless Coke addicts but recovered after therapy at the RC Rehab Center over in Potato Ridge.

And of course, the middle-aged redneck's drug of choice is Preparation H.

## Stranger in a Strange Land

It's a plain fact that drug users can't keep a job.

Whenever we want to impress that fact on our kids, we just point to Herbie the Hippie.

Herbie's never held down a regular job in his whole life. He's kind of a sad figure, really, all alone in the world.

He used to live in Minnesota. Then, in 1969, he heard about the Woodstock Festival and decided to drive to it. But Herbie's brain was so fogged by marijuana that he couldn't read a road map—and he ended up in Woodstock, Georgia, just outside Atlanta.

Well, Herbie kept driving around looking for the other Woodstock until his pink VW microbus blew an engine here in Chicken Neck, Tennessee.

When Herbie first arrived in town he had a long ponytail, an earring, and a little mustache. A lot of people mistook him for Pauline Perkins.

But now he's got a full beard and has been here for nigh onto thirty years, marooned kinda like Gilligan.

Herbie lives in a little abandoned fishing shack out beside Lost Gizzard Lake and grows his own vegetables plus a little "wacky terbacky" for his personal consumption.

Sheriff Gardner knows about Herbie the Hippie's illegal crop, but lets it slide because Herbie never bothers anybody. Pot-heads—unlike crack heads—ain't violent.

In fact, the only trouble we've ever seen out of a marijuana addict happened over in the town of Potato Ridge, thirty miles from here.

This red-eyed, long-haired dude went up to an old woman in a supermarket parking lot, pointed a silver-plated hairbrush at her, and said very slowly, "Okay, lady, keep the cash—just give me all your Twinkies!"

## Surefire Cussin' Remedies

Ivory. Camay. Dial. Irish Spring. Tide. Levi's thirty-four-length leather belt.

# Huntin' and Fishin'

There's an old country saying: "Women do the cookin', men do the hookin'." A man's place ain't in the kitchen, it's on the riverbank.

As soon as your boys get old enough to toddle, take them fishing. It's not just entertainment, it's a survival skill. One of these days they might be out of work and need to fish to feed their families.

Hank Williams Jr. says in one song: "We can skin a buck, and we can run a trot line. / Country folk can survive." That's why every daddy needs to take his kids fishing—even when his wife gets mad because the roof's still not patched and it's about to rain.

Take your children deer and rabbit hunting, too, especially the boys. You don't actually have to shoot the animals. Just getting out in the woods amongst all the wildlife and trees is healthy for kids.

Rufus McKinney goes hunting all the time, and the only thing he's ever killed in his life is a six-pack. He ain't even taken along any ammunition since the drunken day he shot at a buck and bagged his left foot.

Even more shocking, Rufus woke up to find Wiley Watkins trying to mount his foot on the den wall—with Rufus still attached to it.

## When Nature Calls Collect

Unlike Rufus, most rednecks figure the best thing about hunting is that they can drink all the beer they want and the ol' lady ain't there to complain.

They also can take a much-needed leak in the woods and nobody says a word. But be forewarned that peeing outdoors can get dangerous.

Wiley Watkins stopped to relieve himself near the edge of a forest—and peed right on a farmer's electrified fence. Wiley got knocked ten feet and woke up feeling like Ted Bundy that day Florida fried the creep.

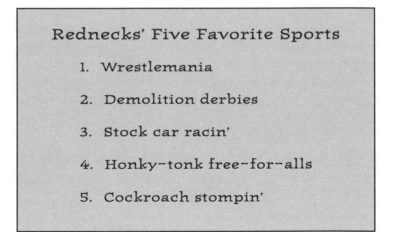

### Rednecks' Five Favorite Sports

1. Wrestlemania

2. Demolition derbies

3. Stock car racin'

4. Honky-tonk free-for-alls

5. Cockroach stompin'

## Guns and Gun Racks

No redneck truck is complete without a gun rack in the rear window and a red, white, and blue bumper sticker that says: GOD, GUNS, GUTS, AND OLD GLORY MADE AMERICA GREAT—LET'S KEEP ALL THREE.

Rednecks love guns, especially hunting rifles. And we don't see anything wrong with letting your young'uns use cap pistols and BB guns to practice shooting. One of these days they might need their skills to defend our nation.

The greatest soldier in World War I was a redneck, Sgt. Alvin York of Tennessee. And the most decorated soldier in World War II was a redneck, Audie Murphy of Texas. That wasn't no accident—it was because redneck boys practice shooting until they can knock the contact lenses out of a gnat's eyes at two hundred yards.

But don't let your kids get hold of your real guns until they're teenagers and can learn how to safely use them. If you catch your little children fooling around with your gun collection, tan their behinds.

Every redneck family's pickup truck ought to have a gun rack in the rear window. However, don't get one if you don't have a truck. Nothing looks tackier than a big gun rack on a Chevy Chevette. Or a bicycle. Or a horse.

A word of warning: Always chain and lock the rifles and shotguns onto your truck's gun rack. Young'uns are naturally curious, and the most curious among them in our neck of the woods are missing a few fingers and toes. We've got nearly grown kids in Mayhew County who can't count past thirteen.

# In-laws and Other Household Pests

It's too bad they don't have a pest control service that comes once a month and sprays your house for unwanted relatives.

Someday these nuisances probably will include your own grown kids.

Once your boys and girls get hitched, don't sell their beds or turn their bedroom into a display area for your prized beer can collection. Most of them are gonna be back faster than you can spell D-I-V-O-R-C-E.

And when your brother-in-law loses his job, he's bound to pile his whole family—including his six dogs—in on you.

Even worse, one day you're sure to have your know-it-all mother-in-law sharing your house after her husband kicks off. Women always outlive men, sometimes because they shoot 'em for foolin' around.

How are you gonna deal with all these extra mouths to feed?

The best way is to secretly change your mealtimes. Get up at three o'clock in the morning, eat all the eggs and bacon in the house, and let your sponging relatives find the refrigerator empty when they drag their lazy butts out of bed later that day.

For supper, bring home a big bag of White Castle cheeseburgers. But leave them in your truck. Have your spouse and younger kids sneak out to the truck, one at a time, to chow down in privacy.

Once your good-for-nothin' "guests" realize you ain't no meal ticket, they'll start looking elsewhere for their grub—and probably move in with some other sucker relative who'll support them.

## Debugging Your Home

It's a little harder to get rid of roaches than relatives. Especially when the bugs are so big that they just laugh at the Orkin man and throw him headfirst out the door.

We've found that Roach Motels work pretty good, but it gets mighty tiresome making up all them little beds every morning.

To get rid of ants, spread boric acid around the house. We don't know exactly why this works. Professor Harland K. Sampson's theory is that that the ants take "acid trips," flee in terror from hallucinations, and bash their little brains out against the wall.

# Junkyards as Vacation Sites

Most young'uns want to go to Disney World—which is fine if you and the family are willing to live on green beans the rest of the year.

Instead of taking out a second mortgage on your trailer to buy Disney tickets, not to mention wearing yourself out with a long drive, consider taking the kids to your own town's most fascinating attraction.

Pack some baloney and tomato sandwiches, pick up enough RC colas for everybody, load the whole family in the car—and head on down to the junkyard!

Car junkyards are a trip back in history. You can show your kids rusting Nashes and crumbling Henry Js, let 'em climb all through humongous Hudsons, and explore the dashboards of DeSotos.

They'll be amazed to see that pickup trucks ain't the only vehicle ever put out by Detroit.

Your brood can play soldiers in old broken-down army jeeps. In a junkyard they'll find loads more places to play hide 'n' seek—in the trunks of cars, under the hood if the motor's been yanked, and in the back of old ice-delivery trucks.

And there's no end to the exciting things that kids can find in a junkyard to take home.

Our boy Lonnie is pleased as punch with the Edsel floor mats on each side of his bed, and our daughter Betty Jean put

**Redneck WRECK-reation park**

up a big Chrysler rearview mirror so she can see to tease the back of her hair. It adjusts from daylight to night vision so she can primp even when the power company cuts off our lights.

Wiley Watkins claims that during his visits to junkyards, he's collected every dashboard cigarette lighter ever made. He says he got a phone call from the Smithsonian Institute begging him to sell his collection to them for over a hundred dollars. Of course, Wiley's prone to stretching the truth until it hollers in pain.

During junkyard junkets, your brood will make memories that will last forever.

Our son Wimpy still talks about the time he stepped on a rusty nail and nearly lost his leg.

His youngest brother, Lonnie, once had to climb a barbwire fence to keep a junkyard dog from ripping him to pieces.

And Earlene Perkins still has a crooked finger from where her brother Junior playfully slammed a '57 Imperial's door on her hand.

How can a dinky little picture of your kids with Minnie Mouse ever compare to unforgettable experiences like that?

---

### Rednecks' Five Favorite Vacation Spots

1. Six Flags over Georgia

2. South of the Border

3. Junkyards with no guard

4. Any fishin' hole

5. Home of out-of-state relative, living or dead

---

## Other Family Outings

When your kids are good, they deserve to get out of the house every couple of weeks.

But you can't always take them for tacos and Cokes, then to

an Elvis film festival. This "eat, drink, and B movie" routine gets stale after a while.

So try a night at the Holiday Inn, which is a big treat for most redneck families. The young'uns will play in the below-ground pool all night, and the parents will finally be able to catch up on their sleep.

Country music concerts are also good family entertainment. Only problem is, big-name singers hardly ever come to our little town.

Little Jimmy Dickens is the only superstar who's been in this area over the past five years, and we had to drive our brood all the way over to Potato Ridge to catch his show.

Come to think of it, the last good concert we saw in Chicken Neck was "Chuck Barris Presents Gene, Gene the Dancing Machine."

We pretty much have to limit our family outings to what's already available in town—and we advise you to do likewise.

• Go around looking at cemetery plots for sale. Tell your kids it's never too early to start planning for the future.

• Take your children to the dog show at the county fair. (And hope your oldest girl doesn't win Best of Show.)

• Drive out by the main highway and watch the kudzu swallow up a tree.

• Take your family to a tractor pull and pull for the smallest tractor.

Don't feel guilty about neglecting housework to take your kids on an outing. As Aunt Alma says, "Sometimes you've got to take time to stop and smell the urinals."

## Rednecks' Five Favorite Actors

1. Chuck Norris (action)

2. Willie Nelson (singin' movies)

3. Fess Parker (historical)

4. John Wayne (war movies)

5. Ned Beatty (romance)

# Keeping Your Kids Safe

We live in a dangerous world these days, and you've got to watch your kids every minute or you'll start losing them right and left.

Here are some precautions you should take:

• Install safety belts in the bed of your pickup truck. They'll keep the young'uns from flying off into the bushes every time you hit a pothole.

Nothing's more aggravating than having to turn around and go back looking for your kids. And the ones you don't find will bug you even more late that night by banging on the door for you to let 'em in.

Why can't kids be like dogs? You put a dog in the back of a pickup and he'll *never* fall out. You can swerve around a curve at ninety miles per hour, and when you look in the rearview mirror your dog will still be there—peeking around the side of the cab with his tongue flapping in the wind and holding up a little sign that says Faster! Faster!

We've never figured out how dogs can hang on when they ain't even got fingers. They must have some magical powers that scientists still don't know about.

That, or else dogs are a whole lot smarter than kids but hide it from you so they can get a free ride through life.

• Before your offspring start riding in your truck, show them how to open and close the bed gate without cutting their hands on the rusted spots.

And don't let them sit close to the brown primer—it'll rub off on their good clothes.

Learning to open the bed gate is extremely important. Over in Potato Ridge a truck plunged into a river and three men riding in the back drowned. Nobody'd ever taught them how to open the gate and they couldn't get out.

• Teach each child how to dial 911 on your rotary phone. If you don't know how to do it yourself, flag down the county constable and get him to show you.

If you ain't got a phone, tell the kids just to holler at the top of their lungs in case of an emergency. A neighbor will think somebody's being murdered at your house and will call the police for them.

• Buy all your girls a big purse so they can carry a tire tool inside at all times.

A heavy iron tire tool is the only handheld weapon that's got more stopping power than a .44 magnum pistol. And it leaves a distinctive head dent that makes it easy for the cops to identify an attacker.

But your girls should be careful about carrying their protection to class, because they could get in trouble. In some redneck areas across the United States, schools have installed sophisticated tire-tool/lug-wrench detectors.

• Make your kids memorize your street address. If they get lost, they'll know exactly where they live.

And when you move, take the house numbers with you so you'll have the same address.

• Drive your son a ways out in the country, dump him off, and see if he can find his way home. If he makes it back, you'll never have to worry about losing him. If he doesn't . . . well, the boy must not have been too bright to begin with. (Rufus calls this the "process of natural selection.")

That might sound a little cruel. But mama birds throw their babies out of treetops onto the hard ground—which has got to hurt a lot more than a little walk.

And don't worry. Somebody will take in your stray kid and give him a good home. Maybe even a better one than the one he was born into.

## Rednecks' Four Favorite Actresses

1. *Sally Field* (*Smokey* movies)

2. *Polly Holliday* (Flo on *Alice*)

3. *Roma Downey* (*Touched by an Angel*)

4. *Dolly Parton* (*Best Little Whorehouse in Texas*)

# Lip-Smackin' Snacks
# for Kids

It's outrageous, but true: These days, cookies and candy cost more than a box of snuff. Moon Pies and Little Debbie cakes are about the only bargains left in stores.

Instead of wasting all that money on store-bought treats, make your own snacks at home using Annie's simple recipes:

• Dip chunks of Spam in candy-apple sauce, stick a toothpick in each chunk, and put a plateful in the refrigerator. They'll go faster than fried peanut-butter-and-banana sandwiches at a convention of Elvis impersonators.

• Whip up homemade carrot candy faster than your kids can say "Bugs Bunny." Just slice some carrots and fry them in butter. Then mix in a batch of brown maple sugar and a little water to make a syrup.

Take the candy out of the skillet and let the sticky coat harden. If your young'uns don't lose all their teeth from eating carrot candy, they'll love it and won't ever ask for Gummi Possums again.

• In the winter, treat your kids to "snow cream"—which is merely ice cream made with snow. Fill bowls with new-fallen snow, pour on some Carnation canned evaporated milk and some sugar, and mix the stuff up real good with a spoon.

One word of warning: Steer clear of scooping snow from anywhere close to the outhouse. You might end up carrying that "all-natural ingredients" craze a bit too far.

• Make your own yummy cookies using graham crackers—which was one of Reverend Billy's greatest inventions ever.

Get a box of cheap store-brand graham crackers and smear some potted meat on them. The crackers will satisfy your kids' sweet tooth. And the potted meat will provide their Recommended Daily Allowances of cooked pork fatty tissue, beef tripe, and vinegar.

---

### Rednecks' Five Favorite Restaurants

1. Denny's (cheap Grand Slams)

2. Shoney's (all-you-can-eat breakfast bar)

3. Stuckey's (yummy pecan desserts)

4. Waffle House (great cheese 'n' onion hashbrowns)

5. Mom's Kitchen, Lake Worth, Florida (try Mike's ribeye steak omelet!)

---

## The Real Dirt on Eatin' Right

Little redneck young'uns also like to eat dirt, and there's plenty of it in the nursery. Go ahead and let 'em chow down—dirt is packed with nutrition!

Rufus McKinney's old lady, Aldie, says she read somewhere that all the minerals a body needs are found in plain old dirt. So why waste money on store-bought "supplement" pills?

But if you live in Georgia, don't let your kids eat too much red clay. It'll clog up their innards and give them such a god-awful case of constipation that you'll have to call Roto-Rooter.

Supplement their dirt intake every now and then with some milk and blackberries to keep 'em in real good shape. Butter-milk's good, too.

One of the healthiest country dishes is "killed" greens. Pick some kale or lettuce, fry a few strips of bacon, and pour the hot grease over the greens. When they wither up like worms on hot concrete, they're ready to eat.

## This Is Your Brain on Fried Eggs

Kids need more than snacks and dirt to keep 'em going after they get past three. And the saying at our house is "Give a damn—give 'em Spam."

To rednecks, Spam is nature's most perfect food. We figure nine out of ten cans of Spam are sold in the South (the other can gets shoplifted in New York City).

There's a good reason Spam is so popular among rednecks. You can fix it more ways than Forrest Gump can fix shrimp, with the comforting knowledge that Spam never wriggled around like them creepy little shrimps do.

The label on a Spam can won't tell you exactly what's inside, but that's only because the makers are afraid their tasty secret recipe will get out and cheap foreign imitations will come pouring into the country.

Now, you've got to be aware that Spam ain't no diet food. Every can contains ninety-six grams of fat. So if your kids are porking up, switch to Spam Lite—which has a mere forty-eight fat grams.

Spam—the unofficial state vegetable of Georgia—can be prepared so many ways it's unbelievable. Here's a sample menu of Annie's daily meals at our house:

**Breakfast**—Cut a can of Spam into quarter-inch slices, slap them in the skillet, and fry until they're turning crispy. Throw in some eggs, fry sunny side up until the edges are brown, and dump the Spam and eggs on your young'uns' plates.

Don't forget that every redneck family's breakfast table has to have a giant jar of apple butter on it. In Tennessee, some parents have been arrested for child neglect because they forgot the apple butter.

And you've got to have hot biscuits and real butter for breakfast—plus a jar of ketchup for the rowdy boys who like to make their Spam look fresh killed.

**Dinner** (which Yankees call "lunch")—Make some cold Spam sandwiches with Wonder Bread, cheap mayonnaise, lettuce, and tomatoes. Serve with grape Kool-Aid.

**Supper** ("dinner")—Finely chop two cans of Spam and mash all the meat together with two eggs (take off the shells first), four ripped-up slices of bread, a chopped onion, and a big bunch of ketchup. Whack the pile into a loaf shape with a big wooden spoon and bake the thing until it's brown on top.

Serve the Spam loaf with canned green beans—Luck's brand if you can get 'em—and mashed potatoes made from scratch.

If you parents would sometimes like to have a romantic dinner at home after getting the kids to bed, light a little birthday candle on the table and treat the two of you to a couple of fine wine coolers.

## Outside Dinin'

Never go to a restaurant that doesn't offer a "value" meal. And if it doesn't have a drive-through window, keep on driving until you find one that does.

Set-down restaurants always cost twice as much (unless it's Denny's). And if the menu's got a fancy tassel hanging from it, add ten dollars per person per tassel inch.

Here's another way to spot expensive restaurants: The name is always misspelled. Never chow down at a place that's got Ristorante or Centre or Olde on the sign outside. You're bound to be overcharged—because if these people can't spell, they sure can't add your bill right.

Rufus McKinney learned the hard way about arm-and-a-leg restaurants. When he drove his family up to Ohio to see his wife's cousin four years ago, he decided to live it up and took them to a highfalutin French restaurant. Big mistake.

Rufus says his kids pigged out on dujour soup and whores devours, and the bill was more than his whole weekly paycheck from the egg-packing plant!

The poor man had to have a Happy Meal to cheer up. (Come to think of it, why does McDonald's have a Happy Meal, but Burger King has a cross san'wich?)

You're more apt to get good prices and good food at a truck stop. Or a restaurant that's got a sign saying Buses Welcome. But be careful if all the buses in the parking lot say State Prison on the side.

Lastly, stay clear of diners that advertise a "family atmosphere." Hell, who wants to put up with kids screaming and grabbing food while you're trying to eat?

# Moonshine and Other Medications

Childhood is a minefield of pesky and even dangerous illnesses. There's not a kid alive who hasn't nearly died from the whooping cough, measles, mumps, the flu, and hundreds of colds.

Why, if we'd kept all the snot our kids blew out of their noses while they were growing up, we'd be able to fill up the town's big elevated water tank.

Which would have made it interesting when the townsfolk took baths.

Of course, dirty ol' Rufus McKinney never woulda noticed.

When your young'uns come down with a cold or the flu, you can buy all kinds of over-the-counter medications down at the Piggly Wiggly market. But that stuff's expensive and usually won't help a bit, so we recommend treating the kids with your own homemade preparations.

Here are some of our favorites, guaranteed to work:

• Dissolve some rock sugar in a warm glass of moonshine, add a twist of lemon if you've got one, and give your kids a little sip to break a fever. Don't let them overdo the sipping, though, or pretty soon they'll start pestering you to bring in a jukebox and will get into a brawl with their brothers.

• Mix up some yellow sulfur and pure hog lard. Smear it on a clear clean cloth to make a poultice, and apply this to your child's chest when she's got any kind of chest cold.

A sulfur-lard plaster also is a cure for athlete's feet on people and the mange on dogs. Maybe even athlete's feet on dogs.

• A good remedy for constipation is a green apple. This will loosen up a kid's innards within minutes, and he'll spend more time in the outhouse than the Sears catalog.

# Home First Aid for Kids

Once your children wear out a snot rag, wash it real good and tear it into strips to use as bandages for small cuts or tourniquets for snakebites or real blood-gusher gashes.

If your kid loses a toe or finger in a bicycle accident, whittle him a new one out of wood. Tape it on the stub and warn him that this time he'd better take care of it!

Do your young'uns have stinking feet? Wash them in bleach and water to kill the smell. Then throw the kid in the dryer and spin him around a few minutes.

A good home treatment for a burn is to slice a cold raw potato and hold it against the burned spot. (Don't try this with a hot french fry.)

To protect your brood's health all year round, give them a big spoonful of castor oil each fall and a dose of cod liver oil every spring.

These awful-tasting preventives are what our parents inflicted on us when we were growing up, and we almost never got sick— or at least admitted it for fear they'd whip out the bottles again.

Another easy preventive is frying all your kids' food in pure lard.

We're convinced that lard and fat keep people from catching colds. Eskimos eat blubber all the time—and we've never in our lives seen an Eskimo with a runny nose.

## Stuttering

Don't worry about it. Mel Tillis's stutter made him a fortune in country music and the *Smokey* movies. Maybe your kid can do the same.

# Nine Greatest Redneck Tragedies

Your kids might expect life to always be filled with fun and games. You've got to warn them to expect a few bumps in the road every now and then—otherwise they'll be completely unprepared when trouble strikes.

So sit down with your young'uns and carefully go over this list of the nine worst calamities that could loom in their future:

1. Loss of a wife.

2. Loss of a cousin (See 1).

3. Loss of a cinder block.

4. Losing a wheel on your home while moving.

5. Watching a deadbeat drive away without paying, sticking you with his bill, while you're on duty at the gas station.

6. Having to sell your coon dog because he's gone deaf and you ain't got the money for a hearing aid.

7. Your pickup truck blows a head gasket.

8. Loss of a husband.

9. Suffering a horrible hemorrhoid attack on a hard church bench.

10. Flicking your cigarette ashes between your legs while sitting on the commode, then realizing the hot ashes didn't hit the water.

11. Losing a show 'n' tell contest at work to see who's got the most teeth.

12. Getting your meat freezer stolen off your front porch.

Redneck's hideaway

# Outhouse Dos and Don'ts

The outhouse is disappearing fast in America, which is a shame because we personally don't believe in indoor bathrooms.

We think it's disgusting that people do their business right down the hall from where they cook their food.

Our outhouse sits proudly on the hill behind our home, and it's been there for over fifty years. Our grandparents used it, our parents used it, we used it, and, God willing, our kids will still be using it long after we've walked through the pearly gates.

Here's what to teach your young'uns about the proper use of the outhouse:

• Don't wipe with a page ripped straight out of the catalog. Crumple up the page over and over until it's soft.

• Always shut the door completely in the wintertime, or else the cold wind will whip inside and leave you with a big icicle on your most private private part.

If you're a girl, people might mistake you for a boy until the icicle melts—and if you're a boy, the girls will stare and flirt.

• On Halloween night, post a guard on the outhouse so juvenile delinquents won't push it over. Grandma's weak bladder makes her go at all hours of the night, and her heart might not be able to take being suddenly horizontal.

• Don't let your sons join their buddies in outhouse races.

This is a game where several teams of kids uproot outhouses and see which team can carry theirs to the town limits first. Problem is, they never take the outhouse holes—and Lord knows who might fall in one of them smelly pits.

Reverend Joshua Boatwright stumbled right into our neighbor's hole one dark night while taking a shortcut home from a tent revival, and we've never heard such language come out of a minister's mouth. We thought he'd been possessed by the devil, or Howard Stern.

## Entertaining in the Outhouse

Going to the little shack out back can be a fun experience if you just listen to our advice:

• Keep reading material in the outhouse so your young'uns can improve their minds while they wait.

But don't leave a *Playboy* out there, or you might never see your sons on weekends.

The *Weekly World News* is a good reading choice for the outhouse. This lively supermarket newspaper is easy to read, lets you keep up with all the latest Elvis sightings, and is a lot more kind to your behind than *Time*'s hard, shiny pages.

• Keep the outhouse furnishings simple and free of clutter. You want your kids to get in and get out as soon as possible, not sit in there and dawdle.

Don't allow the boys to stick sexy Reba McEntire posters on the walls, and don't let the girls put up a mirror to pretty themselves while they're inside. Distractions like that will just lead to squabbles when one kid hogs the outhouse.

Shorty Perkins, who got a bit uppity after buying one-eighth interest in the Swifty gas station, decided to fix his outhouse real fancy. He strung an electrical line out to it and put in a lightbulb. Then he added a frosted globe over the bulb.

Next thing we knew, Shorty had installed a color TV and VCR so his wife, Pauline, could watch her *Love Boat* tape collection while she was on the pot.

Only problem was, Rufus McKinney found out about the color television and started sneaking into Shorty's outhouse to watch the Daytona 500 and other races.

Rufus—who didn't have a TV at that time—would always lock the door. It got to where Shorty and Pauline couldn't even use their own outhouse.

Finally all hell broke loose on the day Shorty got a bad case of the runs—and it just happened to be the same day as the Coca-Cola 600 over in Charlotte. Rufus wasn't about to be disturbed during that big once-a-year event and even brought along his twelve-gauge shotgun to keep away disturbers.

Shorty hung around the outhouse door, banging and begging and looking as agitated as a cow trying to reach a salt lick on the other side of an electrified fence. But Rufus just turned the TV up louder.

So poor Shorty was out of luck, and soon out of clean shorts.

Next day the TV and VCR got sold cheap. Shorty used the money to buy a drawerful of new BVDs and half a case of Imodium A-D.

He posted one bottle on the outhouse door in a little red box that's marked: "Break Glass in Emergency."

## Rednecks' Five Favorite TV Shows

1. *Walker, Texas Ranger*

2. *Hee-Haw* (bootleg videos)

3. *The Andy Griffith Show* (pre-Mayberry, RFD)

4. *The Beverly Hillbillies* (reruns)

5. Fishin' shows featuring country singers

# Putting the X Back in Christmas

Every redneck boy and girl wants a pit bull for Christmas. But these dogs are the "Gift That Keeps on Living," and they'll eat most families out of house and home before the next Christmas arrives.

It's better to give your young'uns a stuffed pit bull. This breed is so bad about attacking people that they often get shot, and you can get a good deal on a carcass if you're in the right place at the right time. (Don't let anybody see your gun.)

Other good presents for kids are gift certificates to fast-food restaurants. Or give them batteries for Christmas, along with a card that says Toy Not Included. They're not going to like any toy you pick out anyway, so make them pay for their own.

The best places to buy Christmas gifts for a wife are gun and knife shows. And if you surprise her with a pistol of her own, don't forget the concealed weapons permit.

Husbands appreciate twelve-packs of beer, another shotgun, and a whoopee cushion for hours of rollicking entertainment down at the bar.

Uncle Billy always buys Aunt Alma romantic stuff for Christmas. We don't know where the heck he got it, but one year he gave her a bottle of French perfume labeled "Eau de Toilette Is Overflowing." The white porcelain bottle was shaped just like a little commode.

A gift the whole family can enjoy is whole-house air conditioning. Look for bargains on used window units and buy one for every room of your home.

Wrap each unit separately in beautiful paper and stack 'em under the Christmas tree. Your kids will be expecting dolls or toy trucks—and boy, will they be surprised!

## The Redneck Stock Portfolio

You want your young'uns to be financially secure when they grow up, so another good Christmas gift is a cow or a pig. They can sell it later on and start building a nest egg for their future.

If you can't afford stock for the holidays, get your kids to invest in a good animal as soon as they start making their own money.

When the market is bullish, kids can lay away a steer at some stockyards and pay only a dollar or so a month on it.

But don't let them invest in billy goat futures. Billy goats ain't got no futures. These danged critters will eat anything—and if your kid's investment gets hold of some spoiled garbage, the market will go belly up.

## Hardheaded Hillbillies in a Software World

More and more kids are asking for computers for Christmas, mostly because they want to play video games.

Our young'uns are growing up in a much more complicated world than the one we grew up in. Scientists have invented so many things—most of 'em too complicated to use—that you just can't keep up with it all.

In Mayhew County the "information highway" is still just a one-lane dirt road where you have to stop and ask directions.

We ain't up to date on computers, slide rules, and other wonders of the twentieth century—and don't really want to learn.

But we think it's time for your kids to know about technology, so we stuck in this section despite not knowing a durned thing about the subject.

Wiley Watkins—who claims to know something about everything—kindly set down and wrote out these definitions of some newfangled technical terms for us. We can't speak for their accuracy since we know Wiley all too well, but here goes:

*software*—Uncle Billy's embarrassing condition when he's had too many beers before hittin' the sack with Aunt Alma.

*hardware*—Assorted stuff, such as metal brackets and electric outlet covers, that you screw all over the outside of your computer to make it look like a junk pile so nobody will steal it. You can buy all you need at a hardware store.

*boot the computer*—What you do when you can't figure out how to turn on the doggone thing. (Tony Lama bull-hides work best.)

*mouse*—Your place of residence. "Wanna eat supper at m'ouse or your'n?"

*RAM*—One of the best pickup trucks ever to come out of Dodge.

*monitor*—An ironclad ship, crewed by a miserable bunch of Yankee lowlifes, that ambushed the proud Confederate ship *Merrimac* during the War between the States.

*on-line*—Where all the cowboys and cowgirls go to when dancing starts at the local honky-tonk.

*upload*—Chug-a-lugging a six-pack in six minutes flat.

*download*—A quick trip to the men's room after all that beer.

*fax*—A husband's version of the night's events when he comes home late. "I had a flat and there wasn't a phone for miles, honey—and them's the *fax!*"

*modem*—A request for extra stuff: "Gimme mo'dem mashed potaters."

*voice mail*—This is where your phone gets cut off for nonpayment and you've got to holler at your neighbor to give her the latest gossip.

*microwave*—A "wave" done by the few fans who attend football games at Chicken Neck Junior College, which hasn't won a single game since 1906. (Although one plucky team did battle Mayhew County Normal School to a 0–0 tie back in '54, giving excited fans cause to tear down the two-by-fours.)

**How a redneck boots his computer**

# Quaint Redneck Superstitions

It's traditional for parents to pass down redneck folklore to their young'uns, and that includes superstitions. Here are some your kids ought to know about:

- If someone sweeps under your feet while you're sitting down, it means you're gonna get married. If it happens twice in the same day, you're going to get shot by her daddy if you don't make that li'l gal your wife.

- If a sweeper hits you with her broom, you're going to jail within a week.

- Don't take along your old broom when you move to a different home. It's bad luck, usually in the form of pesky neighbors who want to borrow every new kitchen appliance you buy.

- When you give someone a knife as a present, put a penny with it to bring the new owner good luck. Rufus McKinney once got a penny with a knife—and only two days later he found three cents in a truck stop urinal.

- Carry bread and salt into your new home for good luck, and also for salt-sandwich snacks in case neighbors drop over to welcome you.

• When you visit somebody, always leave out the same door you came in. Going out another door is real bad luck. Wiley Watkins went out a different door at the courthouse during his divorce trial—and the next morning his wife dropped the divorce.

• If a pregnant woman is big in the butt, she's going to have a little boy. If she's big in the belly, she's going to have a little girl. If she's fat all over, she's going to have three Little Debbie cakes as soon as she gets home.

• Throwing a hat on a table will bring a curse on you. One of the most common is chronic dandruff.

• If a little girl's second toe is bigger than her big toe, it means she'll be the boss when she gets married. This condition is the reason divorcees have to special-order shoes.

# Elvis: Dead or Alive?

One of these nights it's bound to happen: As you tuck your child into bed, she'll look up at you with big, bright, wonder-filled eyes and ask, "Mommy, is there *really* an Elvis Presley?"

What are you gonna say? Tell her Elvis is dead and break her little heart?

No! Don't be cruel. Tell her the truth: The King is alive! ALIVE!!

Every redneck, and lots of nonrednecks, are fully aware that Elvis faked his death back in 1977 so the poor harassed man could go hide out and get some peace. We've seen actual pictures of Elvis riding a motorcycle in Michigan just a few years ago. And on his sixty-second birthday—January 8, 1997—Elvis was spotted in a Social Security line applying for his benefits, according to what we've read.

So when your kid asks about Mr. Presley, just smile and assure her: Yes, my child, there is an Elvis—and one of these days you just might see him in person, gobbling a four-egg peanut butter omelet with cheese hash browns down at the Waffle House!

## Bedtime Stories and Lullabies

The redneck's second Bible ain't a book—it's all the great country songs.

And country music makes wonderful bedtime lullabies. Many songs are so mournful and lonesome that your young'uns will cry themselves to sleep.

A big dose of heartache works twice as fast as Sominex at bedtime, according to Professor Harland K. Sampson.

Just put a radio by your kid's bedside, tune in a country station, and within minutes she'll be sound asleep on her tear-stained pillow.

And you don't have to worry about dirty lyrics. You won't find them in country songs. Our music teaches clean living and respect for women. The only "ho" you'll hear is in "hoedown."

Country songs also will teach your young'uns to respect their parents and to never blame you for the way they turn out. Make sure your kids hear Merle Haggard's great tearjerker "Mama Tried," in which he sings, "Mama tried to raise me better . . . now there's only me to blame, 'cause Mama tried."

Religion and love for animals also are big themes in country songs. The song "Feed Jake" is about a man praying that after he kicks the bucket, his best friend—his dog—will get fed.

With all this inspiring stuff already recorded, why spend time telling bedtime stories or singing lullabies to your kids? You've got better things to do—like making more kids.

## Rednecks' Five Favorite Songs

1. "God Bless the U.S.A." by Lee Greenwood

2. "Stand by Your Man," by Tammy Wynette

3. "Luckenbach, Texas," by Waylon & Willie

4. "Take an Old Cold 'Tater and Wait," by Little Jimmy Dickens

5. Anything by George Jones

# Redneck Toys

Why spend good money buying toys at F. W. Woolworth's and Wal-Mart when kids can entertain themselves for hours with exciting doohickeys found right in their own backyard?

We spent our childhoods floating down the river on inner tubes, swinging off ropes into the ol' swimming hole, and climbing trees.

We had so much fun that sometimes our parents didn't see us for days—which was fine by them because they had plenty of other kids to keep 'em busy.

One time, Glen-Bob walked in the door after a four-day absence and announced, "Mama, I'm home!" She looked up from the kitchen stove and said, "You been gone?"

Here's a list of some of the favorite things we used to do while growing up without a penny in our pockets.

Take a gander at the list and tell your own children to give these pastimes a try. If they're true-blue redneck kids, they'll love these things and will never again ask you to buy 'em a Teenage Mutant Barbie.

• Show your boys and girls how to roll an old tire up and down the road by flicking it with their hand. Pick casings without any worn steel belts popping through, or else the kids will cut their hands and drip blood all over the mashed potatoes at dinnertime.

Also teach them how to curl up inside the tire and

roll down hills. But warn them this can be dangerous. You know that blue Handicapped symbol showing a guy sitting on a circle? Contrary to popular belief, that circle ain't no wheelchair—it's a redneck kid stuck in a runaway tire.

One of the worst things your kids can do is roll down hills they're not familiar with. Wiley Watkins's seven-year-old-son, Jimbo, crawled inside a P215/R70 truck tire and went barreling down Dead Man's Hill just outside of town six years ago, and we ain't seen him since.

Jimbo must be a teenager by now, probably still rolling along.

• Tie a June bug to a thread, hand the string to your son, and let him fly the bug until it gets tangled in his sister's hair. Guaranteed to raise a ruckus.

• Buy your boys a good sharp pocket knife so they can learn to whittle. By watching old men do this at stores, they can learn how to make wooden dolls, little cars and trucks, and long chains with separate links.

After boys get really good at whittlin' with a knife, some irresponsible parents buy them a chain saw so they can carve tree stumps into works of art. We don't recommend that, because artificial limbs are mighty expensive.

• Round up some old washboards and spoons, and show the children how to play tunes on them. It ain't well-known, but this country pastime was the beginning of heavy metal music.

• Put balloons against the spokes of their bicycle wheels so they can pretend they're riding motorcycles. Your kids and their pals can ride around town in a pack and call themselves Heck's Angels.

• Teach your kids to juggle. Have them start with walnuts, then move up to Bud bottles (not your full ones because they might break them) and other objects.

Shorty Perkins's smartest girl, Earlene, even learned how to juggle books—and got hired by a Los Angeles businessman.

## All Their Rowdy Friends

Some smart person once said, "When you're all by yourself, you're in a bad neighborhood." It's true, so encourage your children to make lots of friends.

This is especially important if you live in a place like Chicken Neck—which is such a dull one-horse town that even the horse went off looking for a little action.

Keep your kids busy playing with their pals and you won't have to worry about them. If they get bored, here are three games your young'uns can play with friends:

1.  Snot Blowing for Distance is popular among redneck young'uns, especially if they're all lucky enough to have colds at the same time.

Just get your kids and their friends to line up, press a finger against one nostril, and try to blow snot farther than everybody else. Each little booger gets two tries, one with each nose hole.

2.  Show the young'uns how to build their own kites. Lay out four thin sticks in a diamond shape, add two sticks in a cross shape in the middle, then use string to tie them together at the four places where they cross. Mix some flour-and-water paste to glue a layer of newspapers to the sticks.

Once the paste is dry, attach a long string and your kids have got a one-of-a-kind kite that didn't cost them a red cent.

**3.** Show the kids how to stomp down on a can so hard that it clings to their shoe heel. Then do the other shoe. Let them clomp around the neighborhood to their heart's content.

Yeah, it's noisy, but it's a whole lot cheaper than Rollerblades. Also, the kids won't end up with cracked skulls from slamming into cars or trees.

If a redneck kid gets hurt at your house, his daddy might not sue you—but he sure might shoot you. So the safer the game, the better.

And if the cans get lost or stolen, you're only losing about two cents' worth of recyclable aluminum. Most redneck families find more than that throwed in their front yard every morning.

## Sixteen Uses for an Old Commode

When your commode gets cracked and starts leaking, don't sell it to your neighbor. Your kids can still get lots of enjoyment out of a toilet even after it's useless for the purpose that God intended.

Here are sixteen ways to turn your toilet into a "toy-let":

**1.** Patch up the crack and fill the commode with fresh spring water. Buy some tropical fish and you've got a home aquarium for your youngsters.

An aquarium is educational and lots of fun. The children will spend endless hours watching the cute little

**Redneck go-cart**

fish darting hither and yon, playing with each other, and nibbling cracker crumbs sprinkled on the surface.

And when the kids get tired of watching, give each one a little fishing pole—and let them catch and filet the little suckers to their heart's content!

**2.** Attach a two-foot-square mirror to the back of the tank and let your little girl use the commode as a vanity.

69

She can straddle the lid and use the tank top as a shelf for her makeup and brushes.

**3.** Bolt the commode to old rocking chair rockers and let your young'uns use it as a hobbyhorse.

**4.** Don't have enough chairs in front of the TV? Put a cushion on top of the commode lid and a kid can sit there!

And if you've got a young'un who slouches, the toilet's hard back will straighten him right up.

**5.** If the commode is blue or gold, put a matching fringe around the lid so it hangs down over the bowl. Sew a blue velvet lining around the tank. This creates a little royal "throne."

Your young'uns can use the throne to play King and Queen until they hate each other and have to get a separation.

**6.** Screw four old lawn mower wheels onto a two-foot-square wooden board and bolt the commode down onto the board. Your kids will have the only "commode-mobile" in the neighborhood, and they'll be the envy of all their friends.

**7.** Take the lid out in the backyard and show your boys how to fling it like a discus. Encourage them to compete against other boys.

Next thing you know, your sons will be high school track stars, or else go to juvenile court for breaking neighbors' windows.

**8.** Place the commode in your daughter's bedroom and let her store her dolls inside the bowl and tank.

**9.** Every redneck has to learn how to jiggle the commode handle. Let your kids practice on your discarded toilet. That way they won't damage your new one.

**10–16.** Round up seven old white commode tops and get your kids to paint watercolor Christmas scenes on them. (The white ceramic will look like snow.) Proudly display these works of art in your front windows every Christmas season.

# A Boy's First Truck

A pickup truck is the ultimate redneck toy. And when your son gets old enough to get a driver's license, he's going to start begging you for a truck.

Long before that day, warn him he's got to pay for the vehicle himself. So he'd better get a job by the time he's nine, either running a paper route or mowing yards, and save every penny for that truck.

When he's got about four hundred dollars piled up, take him to look for the truck of his dreams. Don't go to any car lot that features loud, obnoxious salesmen in its TV ads. You know, the ads that blare:

"COME ON DOWN to Al's Used Cars and Trucks! We've got the best deals in town—and we're in business strictly to HELP YOU, not to make money!

"Bad credit? No credit? Runnin' from the law? NO PROBLEM! We can put you in a car faster than they can read you your rights!

"Our prices are cut so low, half our salesmen are on WELFARE! And the little bit o' profit we do make, we send to Mother Teresa!

71

"(Salestaxandtagnotincluded.Offervoidinallforty-eightstates. PlaythisadbackwardandyoucanhearSatan.)"

The best way to buy a used truck is to drive along roads looking for trucks with For Sale signs on them. Especially be on the lookout for a sign that says Husband in Jail—Tow Off His Truck and It's Yours.

Remember, the only things that matter are the engine—which has to be an eight-cylinder—and a straight-drive transmission.

If the engine and transmission are in good shape, you don't care whether the fenders are battered or the upholstery is ripped. Your kid's gonna bang up the fenders anyway, and he can tuck an old blanket over the torn seats.

Once your boy has bought a truck, show him how to pick out the best bald tires for it.

All rednecks—even the womenfolk—know how to fix flats. They don't just run out and buy new tires when the tread gets a little worn down. And they almost never pay more than twenty dollars for a set of tires, including balancing and a spare.

These days whitewalls are nearly as cheap as black walls, so your son can spiff up his truck with fancy-lettered tires for just a few pennies more.

Usually the first things to quit on an old truck are the windshield wipers. Show your boy how to tie two long pieces of twine to the wiper on the driver's side and run one string in each window. Then tie them together inside the cab.

By pulling the twine back and forth, he can work the wiper good enough to get home on a rainy night.

A redneck's truck ain't complete without mud flaps. The most prized ones have a drawing of Yosemite Sam with a big pistol in each hand and snarling, "Back off!"

Your boy can make his own set of mud flaps by cutting

squares out of a neighbor's porch carpet while they're away bowling or vacationing at the junkyard.

---

### Rednecks' Five Favorite Pickup Lines

1. "I can carry forty bales o' hay in this baby."

2. "What's yore sign? Mine says, '0 to 60 in 20 minutes.' "

3. "Look, honey, the new Bondo matches yore dress!"

4. "Sure, she's slow, but the radio works real good."

5. "You can keep the kids, but *I* get the damn truck!"

---

## A Boy's First DUI

Call AAA to pick up the truck. Call AA to pick up your boy. Sell the damn truck.

# School Days, Rule Days

Like it or not, kids have to go to school. Most students think the purpose of school is to educate them. But the real secret purpose is to give their parents a badly needed break from child rearin' a few hours a day.

Check your American history books and you'll discover this whole school system scheme was cooked up by politicians who were parents. Coincidence? You be the judge.

Here are the rules you need when your young'uns get into school:

• Never send your son to his fourth-grade class without a good clean shave. Or your daughter either, for that matter.

Nothing looks worse on a grade school young'un than a five o'clock shadow—it kinda resembles a hog that's been slaughtered and shaved but still has short bristles sticking out of its hide.

And if you let your boy go to school without shaving, the teachers will poke fun at him—especially if they're one of those fuzzy-faced, four-eyed Yankee teachers who've sashayed down to the South on a "mission" to educate our kids. Next thing you know, your kid will beat up the teacher and wind up in a heap of trouble.

• Before your kids take off for school in the morning, always check their shoes.

If they're still half asleep, you can almost bet they'll

**Typical redneck sixth-grade class**

put on a black shoe and a brown one. That would be fine if the young'un was just going down to the store. But he's got to learn that for formal occasions, such as school, he's got to wear the same color shoes.

It's a good idea to remind your brood every now and then that their pair of brown shoes is for school, their black pair is for church.

• When the kids get home from class, teach them to take off their shoes as soon as they hit the front porch.

Grade-schoolers under age twenty should always go barefoot when playing after school, up until the time they start coming inside with frostbite on their toes.

Going shoeless in winter and summer makes your kids grow up healthy and hardy, saves shoe leather, and keeps them from tracking dog poop into the house.

Redneck kids can't smell. If a boy's got his shoes on and steps in a pile of hound droppings, he won't even notice it. He'll come squishing right through your front door leaving stinky tracks all over the floor.

And sooner or later, some visitor to your house will notice the tracks.

• To save money, pack your kids' school lunches. Don't get fancy—just give each one a can of Vienna sausage, potted meat, or sardines. Throw in a few packs of crackers, which you can pick up free at restaurant buffet bars.

## The Birds, the Bees, and the Backseat

School-age redneck boys are naturally interested in girls. It's in their jeans.

And redneck girls are just as curious about boys, although they try harder not to show it.

But it's up to you parents to teach your boys and girls about the ways of romance, how to behave on dates, and (when they're older) safe sex.

We realize you don't want to even *think* about sex and your kids. But it's something you'll have to face sooner or later. None of us got on this earth because our parents just kissed and held hands on the front porch swing.

Problems can crop up with teenagers no matter where they go on a date—to the drive-in show, the Saturday night rodeo, a tractor pull, wrestling at the town auditorium, or parking out by the lake.

When a boy takes a girl to the drive-in and he's got a cold, nothing's more embarrassing than having a runny nose all night. Snot also makes popcorn taste terrible, and trying to pass it off as "buttered" popcorn won't work with a lot of girls.

So tell your boys that in an emergency, their truck's gas cap rag can be used as a snot rag.

Some parents buy books advising them how to tell their kids about sex. But the easiest way to teach young'uns is to take them to a farm where they can watch the cows, pigs, and other creatures in action.

Chances are that once your daughter see what a cow has to go through while giving birth to a calf, she'll *never* let a boy touch her indecently!

## Sex, Lies, and Duck Tape

We used to have a little town tramp named Lisa who spent more time in the backseat than that little dog with the bobbin' head in the rear window.

If your daughters turn out like Lisa, we pity you—because she was a laughingstock from one end of Chicken Neck to the other. All the boys called her Moaner Lisa.

She was a preacher's daughter, but she sure didn't act it. Lisa guzzled beer like a man dying of thirst, swore like a sailor, and lied more than all the town's lawyers put together.

Even worse, as she got older she got into something called "bondage." Lisa would get a boyfriend to tie her up with duck tape before she'd agree to do it with him. She got some kind of thrill out of that.

Next thing we knew, Lisa had left Chicken Neck and was working at the Chicken Ranch out in Las Vegas. On the side she became the spokeswoman for Tru-Tite duck tape.

That ain't no fitting end for any girl. Tell your daughters the sad story of Moaner Lisa and maybe they'll keep their clothes on, at least more often.

# Twins: Should You Keep Just One?

The problem with having twins is that they're twice as costly to raise. And if you've seen one twin, you've seen the other—so why keep both?

A family of kids should all look different so the parents can tell right away who did something wrong. You can't tell twins apart unless one is a boy and one is a girl—and you still might get confused if the boy happens to be a tad sissy.

So if you've got a married sister who yearns for young'uns but can't have any, why not give her one of your twins? Then you and your sister will have a matched set!

We realize most parents are going to want to keep both twins for themselves. If that's what you decide, you should do certain things to make sure you can identify which kid is which.

Shave one twin bald, and let the other grow long hair. Have them switch styles every New Year's Day.

Get a barber to cut each twin's name on the back of his head. You still won't be able to tell them apart when they're facing you, but when one is running away after some mischief you can holler real loud, "James Edward, you GIT RIGHT BACK HERE!"

Make one twin learn Spanish and speak it all the time. You won't understand a word she's saying, but that's okay—most kids' chatter ain't worth listening to anyway.

Feed one twin more than the other. At family reunions you

can introduce them as: "This here's my boys Jimmy and Johnny—Jimmy's the fat one with the Big Mac wrapper stuck between his teeth."

# Use and Care of
# Snot Rags

Every boy should carry a handkerchief in his back pocket. It's got all kinds of useful purposes—you can wipe a runny nose, clean dog poop off your shoes, and tie up loose hard candy in it.

Snot rags should be colored, not white, and have patterns so snot boogers won't show. It's downright embarrassing for the teacher or preacher to compliment your young'un on his pretty polka-dot snot rag, then take a closer look and learn the awful truth.

Teach your kids to clean their handkerchiefs at least once a year, usually in the spring. The easiest way is to stick the rag on a fishing hook and swish it around in a river or lake.

Last May our boy Lonnie cast his snot rag out in Lost Gizzard Lake and caught a six-pound snot-lovin' bass!

We gave it to Rufus McKinney. He likes exotic foods.

# Vaseline's Role
# in Rearin'

We wish Vaseline came in fifty-gallon steel drums, because it's the handiest product that parents can buy.

You can slap this gooey stuff on a baby's crotch to ease the pain of diaper rash . . . smear it inside your kids' too-tight shoes so they won't get chafed heels . . . stick it up their red, burning nose holes when they've got colds . . . and dab it on their lips to soothe winter cold sores.

Parents can use Vaseline to oil their guns cheap, to stop doors and beds from squeaking, and to ease their awful suffering from hemorrhoids.

WD-40 works good on doors and beds, too, but we don't advise spraying it on your burning butt.

Vaseline's also important for grooming. Boys can comb the goop through their hair for that slicked-back Elvis look still prized in redneck country.

## Sideburns for Young'uns
## under Ten

Boys of all ages love sideburns, but unfortunately the little ones can't grow them. So as your dogs shed hair, sweep it up and give it to your small sons. They can use Elmer's Glue to paste the fur on their cheeks.

Some kids make real-looking sideburns this way. But a few others botch the job and end up looking like Wolf Boy—which can be a plus if Halloween's just around the corner.

## More Grooming Tips

Once a year, take each kid in for his tooth cleaning.

Don't let your boy use Skoal until he's got two teeth.

Buy each of your girls a can of 10W-30 motor oil so they can keep their hair shiny like the boys do with Vaseline.

And when your young'uns get close to being grown-ups, clip out the following chapter—and tell them to follow these simple directions for living the redneck life.

## The Little Redneck
## Instruction Book

Always have a cigarette dangling from the corner of your mouth, even in church. Even if you're a woman. Even if you're the preacher.

Learn to smoke like a redneck. Hold the filter between your thumb and forefinger, with the other fingers cupped over it.

Never use a truck's ashtray—open the window and flick the ashes outdoors where they belong.

If you chew Skoal or Beech-Nut while driving, spit the juice out your own window. Some rednecks like to show off by spitting all the way across the seat and out the passenger-side window. That can get mighty messy for riders, especially if the window happens to be rolled up.

Don't wear your false teeth except on formal occasions or when you're trying to pick up girls.

Keep a pink or powder blue leisure suit in your closet to wear to weddings, funerals, and the annual PTA dance.

Never buy fancy bottled water with a foreign-sounding name on the label. For the price you pay for a sixteen-ounce bottle of this stuff, you could buy a whole six-pack of Old Milwaukee. If you want to carry water around with you, get a gallon milk jug and fill it up at the store's water machine for a dime or a quarter.

Your belt buckle has to be solid silver and at least a half-inch bigger than your billfold. Some rednecks pay more for their buckle than they do for their pickup truck.

Get your first name or nickname burned or stitched onto the back of your belt. That way it'll always be returned to you if you happen to lose it. (You might want to deny ownership if your belt is found in the backseat of some redneck's wife's car.)

Don't join a gym. Most rednecks get a real workout on the job and don't need no costly gym membership. Besides, they'd rather jump off an interstate bridge than wear them short silky gym shorts.

Never go to a tanning bed. People pay to use these contraptions even in Florida—which is the Sunshine State, for God's sake! If for some crazy reason you want to tan your body, just smear butter or lard all over yourself and lay out in the backyard.

Learn to pick a guitar, a banjo, and your nose.

Never wear color-coordinated clothes. Rednecks' shirts and caps are always different colors. If you show up on the job site wearing the same color shirt and cap, the foreman will send you home to change.

If you've still got your high school jacket with the football letter on it, drag it out and start wearing it again in your forties and fifties. You can get sympathy from gals by telling them you're just eighteen, but you've got that aging disease progeria.

# Weighing Kids
# on Store Scales

Why pay good money for a home scale when every supermarket's got one in the produce department?

Just put your baby on the scale and see how much she's gained. Ignore women shoppers who come up to you and ask, "What aisle is the babies on?"

When your kids get bigger, you can weigh them on truck scales out by the highway.

Drive over the scales with the kid in your truck, then dump him beside the road and go through again. Subtract the second figure from the first and you've got your young'un's weight, give or take a diaperful.

## Child Rearing for Peanuts

With prices going up every day, it's getting harder and harder for parents to stretch their dollars. Here's a few suggestions that might help you save money:

**Beds**—Seems like every week you pick up your neighbor's discarded newspaper and read that some hotshot movie actress has spent fifty thousand or more on her new baby's bed.

Well, folks, stars can do that because they've got more money than John spoke about. But redneck parents can't be so extravagant. Most of us here in Chicken Neck have to watch every penny we spend.

We're not saying our town is poor, but some people can't wait to get on jury duty because it means a pay increase.

So instead of buying a costly bed for each of your kids, do like we do: Go out to a flea market or yard sale and spend a couple of bucks on a big old beat-up chest of drawers.

Take out the drawers and slap down a layer of foam rubber bedding in each drawer. Throw in a quilt and pillow and— bingo—you've got a whole roomful of beds!

You can chop up the rest of the chest for kindling wood.

**Toothpaste**—For the price of a tube of toothpaste these days, you could buy two tickets to the county fair and have enough left over to dunk the smart-mouthed clown.

Some of the most expensive brands are the ones with baking soda in them, and that's just plain funny. We were raised brushing our teeth with baking soda—the box kind, not the fancy tube kind—and now it's fashionable!

You can get a box of Arm & Hammer baking soda for pocket change. That box will last for months—even if your kids religiously brush their teeth every two weeks.

**Shampoo**—When kids get around to finally washing their hair, they always slap on too much shampoo. So buy the cheapest brand, something not seen on TV.

If you buy a TV-advertised product, you're just helping pay the salaries of all those beautiful models with "lustrous, shining, glorious hair."

After buying a bottle of bargain shampoo, pour half of it into an empty bottle and fill both up with water. You'll have two bottles for the price of one!

Thriftiness is a way of life in our family. Aunt Alma's still using a bottle of White Rain shampoo she bought in the fifties. And she's the only person we know who still Minipoos her hair.

**Groceries**—One way to save on your food bills is to starve your kids all weekend, then take 'em to a cheap "all you can eat" buffet restaurant on Sunday night. Your young'uns will go into a feeding frenzy, and hopefully you can hustle them out the door before the owner calls the cops.

## The Britches of Mayhew County

Let the uppity city kids keep their neatly pressed designer slacks and pointy Italian shoes. When you're rounding up pants and other duds for your young'uns, be sensible and cheap.

**Britches**—Buy used Levi's, Lee's, Wrangler, and Dickies work pants. They're the only britches that can be legally sold in Mayhew County, thanks to a 1959 law passed by the county commission.

These brands will wear forever and you never have to iron 'em. We bet that if anybody tried to open a laundry business specializing in pressing Levi's, the fool would go out of business in an hour.

**Footwear**—Always buy shoes two sizes too big and let your kids grow into them. If the shoes flop around too much on their feet, stick pieces of cardboard behind their heels.

When your boys and girls get older and start whining for boots, find them a cheap pair at a yard sale. That'll have to do until they start earning money and can buy fancy boots made from the skins of rattlesnakes, ostriches, alligators, or roadkill.

**Hats**—When buying hats for your young'uns, you've got only two choices: bill caps or cowboy hats.

Pick a cap with a slogan on it. The most prized is a "Cat hat"—one that says Caterpillar on it. Funeral home caps run a close second. Rednecks wouldn't give you a dime for a cap with a polo club emblem.

The average redneck keeps a selection of caps at home, at

work, behind his truck seat, and in the outhouse. We know people who've got more caps than IQ points.

Don't buy your young'uns a beret. Rednecks would rather get caught naked in a gay bar than be seen wearing a beret in public. Even Big John Wayne looked kind of sissy wearing one in *The Green Berets.*

**Socks**—White-sock makers would be out of business if it wasn't for rednecks and tennis players. That's the only color we ever buy—because they show the world we've got clean feet.

If you send your kid to school wearing colored socks with fancy patterns, you're just asking for him to get ridiculed. You might as well put big yellow clown shoes on him.

The only time rednecks wear black socks is when they've got on white shoes. We're big on "contrast."

**Neckties**—No self-respecting redneck young'un would ever own a necktie. If they need one for a wedding or some such nonsense, send 'em down the street to borrow one. Or slap a curtain sash around their neck and cut it to the proper length.

## Night of the Living T-shirt

When it's warm, redneck kids like to sleep buck-naked until they're maybe ten years old. And when they need something to wear at night in winter, there's no need to blow a wad on fancy name brand pajamas or nightgowns.

Your old T-shirts will do just fine. If your potbelly or bosom stretched them out a bit, so much the better.

Rufus McKinney's potbelly is so big he can stand in two zip codes at once, and young teenagers go wild over his T-shirts. Sheriff Gardner says they've got a street value of one hundred fifty dollars each.

'Course, they've got to be washed six or seven times because they're so dirty. And the Lord only knows what little invisible critters might be living on 'em. We've heard that when Rufus takes off a T-shirt at night, it crawls all by itself into the closet.

Look around malls and streets these days and you'll see that kids love the "baggy" look. They don't even realize that rednecks have been wearing baggy ripped clothes since the beginning of time.

We were "grungy" when "grungy" wasn't cool.

Give your older boys pocket T-shirts so they'll have a place to keep their Marlboros. If the T-shirts don't have pockets, show them how to roll up the cigarette pack in the left sleeve.

If you ain't got any extra T-shirts, toddle down to a Goodwill or Salvation Army thrift shop and buy a bunch for a quarter apiece.

Don't be embarrassed to buy secondhand clothes. We've heard of people paying fifty dollars for a pair of prewashed jeans, which is pretty dumb. It makes more sense to let the first owner prewash the jeans, then later you can buy them at a thrift shop for two bucks.

Mind-boggling treasures can be found tucked away in flea markets and secondhand stores. We make the rounds about once a month, and it never ceases to amaze us what precious things people throw away.

Last week we bought a genuine Little Jimmy Dickens—1995 World Tour T-shirt for a dime, and you could barely see the ketchup and mustard stains on it.

Our girl Betty Jean grew up sleeping in a See Rock City—Atop Lookout Mountain T-shirt that she still owns to this day. She's got it framed and hanging on her bedroom wall, just above the yellow lava lamp she's had since the sixties.

As for our son Lonnie, his favorite bedtime T-shirt is one he found lying in the middle of Old Muskrat Road four miles outside of town.

It says Lonnie's Hubcap Heaven and has a drawing of St. Peter with a smiley hubcap face, welcoming two flattened hubcaps at the pearly gates.

## Buying Brand-New Duds

We've got so many stringbean boys in our town that the local 7-Eleven opened a Tall and Skinny clothing section. We hope this idea catches on nationwide so all parents can save on new garb.

Wherever you shop, never take the price tag off a shirt or pair of jeans until you're absolutely sure your young'un will keep it. If the shirt gets too tight after a few washings, or the jeans chafe a kid's crotch, you'll need the tag to return it.

Of course, this means you'll have to wash these clothes by hand while holding the tag above the water. But that's better than losing money.

Why do you think Minnie Pearl kept the price tag on her hat for years? It's because she planned on returning it someday. (Hopefully there's a Refunds and Exchanges desk in heaven.)

## Manners

This shouldn't take a lot of work on your part, because redneck boys and girls just naturally have good manners. It's in their jeans.

Usually the first word out of a redneck baby's mouth ain't "Mama," it's "Ma'am." (Except for Rufus McKinney's fat little boy, Elmer—his first word was "Spam.")

You can learn a lot about teaching a kid to be courteous by

watching *The Andy Griffith Show*. You'll see that little Opie is always polite and well-mannered.

Opie never gets out of line because he wants to make his daddy, Sheriff Andy, proud of him—and because Deputy Barney always carries that dreaded one bullet with Opie's name on it.

*The Andy Griffith Show* also is a lesson in how *not* to raise your kids:

- Don't let 'em get away with throwing rocks, like Ernest T. Bass—who broke windows all over Mayberry and never once got any serious punishment for it.

- Keep 'em away from hard liquor so they won't end up the town drunk, like Otis.

- And don't let 'em change their name and become a sneaky lawyer, like Sheriff Andy did later in life.

Raise your boys and girls with love and they'll turn out fine.

But if by chance one of your young'uns ever starts to become a little smarty-pants, don't waste time putting that whippersnapper straight with a hickory switch.

Show your young'uns that Mama and Daddy care enough about them to whup their little butts!

## Courtesy

Manners and courtesy go hand in hand. Teach your children to hold doors open for little old ladies, pop the caps off beer bottles for gals, and courteously swerve to just barely nick jaywalkers instead of flattening them like pancakes.

When you take the young'uns for a drive, point out that pickup truck drivers are the most courteous people on the road. Ever notice that when you're trying to get out from a side street onto a crowded highway, it's always a pickup man who slows down and waves you out?

A guy in a Mercedes won't ever do that. He's too busy talking on his car phone while rushing to his business appointments, and slowing to let you out might cause him to be three seconds late.

If you want to get away from blaring horns, head out into redneck country. Rednecks almost never honk their horn unless it's to get a cow or a drunk jaywalker off the road—or just for fun, to aggravate some jerk on a car phone.

Your kids also should be raised to believe in fair play, something that's ingrained in every redneck.

If you don't believe it, trying bullying some little guy in a redneck bar. You'll find yourself tackled by six good ol' boys and you'll wake up outside in the gutter—with your teeth still inside the bar, talking to your missing ear.

An experience like this can scar you for life. Luckily people in Mayhew County who've lost ears in bar fights and fingers in gun accidents can get help by joining a local support group, Parents without Parts.

# X Marks the Pot

Ever wonder why rednecks keep an old commode in their front yard? It's so their kids, playing outside at night, won't have to keep running inside to pee.

This outside pot's also a courtesy for neighbors who can stop to relieve themselves while reeling home from the bar late at night.

But most redneck yards are just high weeds. To make the commode easier to find, put a five-foot stick beside it.

You might also want to mark the old couches and cars in your yard so kids won't trip over them.

While you're at it, stick a couple of posts on either side of your driveway—which in most redneck neighborhoods is just two tire tracks through the weeds.

## Redneck Home Furnishings

Sooner or later your daughters will be living in a home of their own (hopefully, not a home for unwed mothers), and they've got to learn how to decorate the inside as well as the yard.

They might choose to furnish their house like yours, but then again they might want the place to look respectable.

Redneck home decor might not always be classy, but it's definitely in a class of its own. Instead of hiring a decorator, just have your daughter follow our suggestions:

• Bowling trophies should always be placed in your home's front windows, not in the shower or on top of the commode. Few sights are as awesome as driving down a redneck street and seeing all the bowling trophies gleaming in the sun.

• Hang a pair of genuine longhorn steer horns on the wall near the front door. Visitors can flip their cowboy hats onto the horns as they come inside. Don't let anybody throw his hat on a table—this will bring you bad luck.

• Above your couch, place a big framed picture of a soaring bald eagle and a framed collection of Indian arrowheads. A black velvet painting of John Wayne would really set off your wall decor.

• Before visitors come over, check the couch to make sure no springs are sticking out. If you find one showing, push it back down and cover the hole with two layers of duck tape.

• The best decoration for your coffee table is a bronze Western sculpture by Frederic Remington—who was the world's greatest artist except for Norman Rock-well.

Rufus McKinney has a beautiful Remington sculpture with a brass plate that says End of the Trail. It shows a weary Indian on a weary horse, with his spear pointed down to the ground.

We don't know if the sculpture is authentic or not, because the Indian is wearing a Washington Redskins jacket and the artist's signature reads Freddie Remmington. But it sure is a conversation piece.

• Keep your ironing board set up in the kitchen. It can be used as an extra table when too many relatives drop over for supper.

• Keep a spare roll of toilet paper under a pink knit cover on the commode tank top. You don't want people dirtying up your hand towels in the worst way.

• Nail some tin sheets on the roof over your bedroom. Rain beating on a tin roof is the coziest sound in the world and you'll sleep like a baby.

• Put a bug zapper in every room. Especially the bathroom.

**Redneck's bunkbed**

# Young'uns Gotta Work

Don't give your kids allowances. That's just childhood welfare!

You've got to slave long hours for your money—make your young'uns do the same.

Allowances only teach kids they can get somethin' for nothin'. They'll grow up expecting a handout from the family or the government and won't be worth a warm bucket of spit.

If they want a couple bucks for themselves, put 'em to work around the house. Or tell them to walk down the street asking neighbors if they need something done.

Neighbors always can use wild blackberries—which are delicious when covered with sugar and milk. In early summer, put your kids to work picking blackberries to sell around the neighborhood.

Tell them to wait until the berries turn from green to red to black before they start picking. Only Yankee tourists will buy red berries—they're easily convinced that they're getting "mountain strawberries."

## The Man with the Goal 'n' Gun

Kids have to have goals in life, or they're going to just drift along jobless and wind up eating out of Dumpsters.

Maybe that's an okay life for a single man or woman, but not when you're married. It's downright embarrassing for a friend to catch you, your wife, and kids all chowing down on day-old Grand Slams behind Denny's.

You might try to tell the friend you're just having a family picnic and the park was too crowded, but the odds are only about fifty-fifty that he'll believe you.

That's why chores are so important to a kid. They teach your young'uns that if they want to have all the good things in life—such as a 30.06 hunting rifle or a silver-plated ladies' derringer—they've got to work for them.

## Callus Behavior

Look closely at America's rednecks and you'll see that most of us are fairly smart and not the least bit afraid of hard work.

Redneck men and women are proud of the calluses on their hands—it's part of our culture. In fact, the word "redneck" comes from us working out in the hot sun and getting burned on the neck. And calluses are our badges of honor.

Now, in the nonworking crowd it's a different story.

A 1994 study by Professor Harland K. Sampson of Chicken Neck Junior College showed that among America's nonworkers, there are only 3.7 hand calluses per 100,000 people—and 89 percent of the calluses come from opening and closing the mailbox looking for government checks.[2]

But just like any group in America, the redneck nation includes a few shiftless folks. Some are so lazy that if they saw a dollar lying in the street, they'd ask somebody to pick it up for them.

One of our neighbors (we'll call him Charlie J. to hide his identity, because he might not appreciate this publicity) is too lazy to even remove his cowboy hat when he goes to bed.

2. Professor Harland Konan Sampson, "Social Significance of Dermal Thickening in the General Populace," *New England Journal of Calluses,* vol. XXII (June 7, 1995): 6.

One night he was fidgeting around in bed, and when his wife asked what was wrong, he said, "I sho' wish somebody would take this hat off my head."

Charlie's wife flicked it off . . . and learned to her shock, after six kids and twenty-three years of marriage, that her husband was bald.

The only job Charlie ever held in his life was a six-month stint at a hot dog stand outside the Trailways bus station. And even though he worked by himself, he never once got voted Employee of the Month.

To Charlie's credit, one month he did come in third in the voting.

Another family over in Potato Ridge (we'll call them the Johnsons, since that's their real name) must have inherited a laziness gene. They moved so slow that beside them, a snail looked like it had blazing Olympic speed.

When cable TV came to town, the Johnsons signed up for the home shopping network so they wouldn't have to bother going to the store. But after watching for two weeks they never saw a single sale on beans or grits, so they canceled their cable.

Don't tolerate such laziness in your own family. Hard work is a redneck tradition—and your kids have to carry on that proud tradition.

## Picking the Right Job

Most young'uns don't know what they want to be when they grow up. It's up to you to help steer them into a career.

While Rufus McKinney was raising his six kids during America's moon shot era, all six wanted to work at Cape Canaveral. But frankly, none of them were rocket scientists. So Rufus got them all jobs working with him at the egg-packing plant.

When your young'uns hit the terrible teens, teach them to avoid these three phrases that could screw up their chances of getting their first job:

"Welcome, Kmart shoplifters."

"Today's red light special is on aisle four. And remember, you must be completely satisfied!"

"Would you like flies with that?"

Don't expect your kids to keep their first job for life. Most people have to try different occupations before they find the one that suits their special talents.

Polly Puckett, who lives four doors from us, was born with six fingers on each hand. That kinda made her famous in town, but she couldn't seem to turn her celebrity status into a lasting job.

Poor Polly flunked out as a typist, a masseuse, and a chicken plucker before Sheriff Gardner finally found her the perfect job. He made her a deputy on his DUI task force.

Every time Polly pulled over a drunk driver, she'd show her hands and say, "How many fingers am I holdin' up?" Naturally the stewed guy would guess, "Uhh . . . ten?"

Polly cleared the roads of so many sloshed drivers that she was named Officer of the Year by MADR (Mamas Against Drunk Rednecks.)

## Shorty's Rise to Riches

Alan Jackson's song "It's All Right to Be Little Bitty" expresses our feelings exactly. If your young'uns are satisfied with their lot in life and don't set their goals too high, they'll be happier.

You can use Shorty Perkins as a good example of somebody who aimed too high and kept shooting himself in the foot. He wasted half his life trying every money-making scheme he could concoct, but nothing worked.

One time he tried to talk Sheriff Gardner into making 911 a 900 number and splitting the profits. Shorty's plan was to advertise, "Only $1.29 per minute on your hospital bill." The sheriff gave him the boot.

Next, Shorty came up with the idea of telemarketing for 7-Eleven. But nobody wanted to buy Slim Jims and Slurpees by mail, even when he offered next-day delivery.

After Widow Brown's indoor toilet got stolen, Shorty tried to market a homemade antitheft device that beeped and said in a computerized voice, "Please back away from the commode. You are too close. Please back away."

The widow bought the first one. But the doggone thing went haywire and started talking in the middle of the night—and she shot her commode to death so she could get to sleep.

When the traveling carnival came to town, Shorty opened a booth that featured "dancing chickens." He had a cage with a hot plate as the floor, and when he turned up the heat the chickens would do the jitterbug like crazy.

Shorty billed his carny dancers as Poultry in Motion.

But one night he got distracted while the heat was on high—and next thing we knew he was billing his star performers as Shorty's Southern Fried Chicken.

His financial picture got so dim that during one low period his wife Pauline's false teeth got repossessed. She's such a bigmouth that the dentist had to send a tow truck—and billed poor Shorty for that, too.

Shorty finally hit it big when he bought one-eighth interest in the gas station. And when the money started coming in, he began living well just to impress people who figured he'd never make it.

He bought himself a tacky toupee that looked like roadkill sitting on top of his head, a double-wide trailer, a big above-ground pool, and one of them fancy foreign-made Rolodex watches.

But Shorty still stuck with his bigmouthed, nagging wife—which is proof to your kids that money can't buy happiness.

**Rednecks' intellectual pursuit**

# Dumb and Dumber

Sadly, as with in any group in the USA, the redneck world includes a handful of people who are dumber than dirt. As Aunt Alma would say, "They ain't got all their marbles lined up in a row."

When Rufus McKinney's son Elmer tried to enlist in the army, they asked him what his IQ was and he said, "Twenty-twenty!" For some reason Elmer got turned down, but his sharp "I" did get him a job as a quality inspector down at the egg-packing plant.

Like laziness, dumbness seems to be passed down from one generation to the other in certain families around here.

Some people in our town have looked up their family tree and seen their second cousins still living in it.

And got hit in the eye by a beer can being tossed down.

We know one family so dumb they celebrate Independence Day and the Fourth of July on different days.

Sadly, we've got dogs around here with higher IQs than their owners. That ain't no joke—it was proven by Professor Sampson in a scientific master/pet study at Chicken Neck Junior College in 1990.

One backwoods bloodhound owner scored so low that Professor Sampson told him he'd be better off getting a brain transplant. We heard the man seriously considered having his brain swapped for a monkey's brain in an operation that would have made headlines across the county.

But the deal fell through because the monkey wanted ten dollars' difference.

# Zero Tolerance for Misbehavin'

Don't you just want to puke when you see all them whining teenagers on daytime talk shows blaming their parents for all their problems?

On one show this pimply faced drug fiend claimed her problem was her parents' fault because they made her clean up her room as a kid. Our neighbor Rufus got so mad at that, he took his twelve-gauge off the wall and blasted the TV!

Now Rufus has to look all over town for a TV to watch the car races, which is an inconvenience he blames on that stupid girl.

Rufus raised three boys and three girls and they all turned out right because, like us, he taught his kids responsibility.

Here's the most important rule: *Don't let kids get away with nothin'!* Early in life, teach them to take the blame for whatever they do.

When your little girl kicks you under the table and won't stop, thinking it's funny, kick her back. Don't be vicious—kick just hard enough to show her how it feels.

If your two-month-old throws up on your shoulder, make her clean it up. If she wets her bed, make her wash and dry the sheets. Don't accept excuses, such as she ain't learned to walk yet.

And if your little son burns down your house while playing

with matches, go borrow some tools and make him build you a new one—with a Jacuzzi this time around.

It might take him twenty or so years, but you can bet that young'un will never touch a match again the rest of his life.

And when your boys get old enough to drink alcohol, teach them to drink responsibly. That means paying for their own beer instead of sneaking it onto a buddy's tab.

## Passing Out Chores

Plenty of redneck families put out their own vegetable gardens. Assign your boys to do the planting and hoeing, and get your girls to shuck the corn and break the green beans.

Mamas shouldn't let daughters get away with layin' in front of the TV while you do all the housecleaning. Switch off the set, boot their lazy butts off the couch, and put 'em to work.

Your home should have a chore list. Give your kids the choice of either volunteering for a daily job or choosing one at random by pulling a slip out of a "chore jar."

In the chore jar, put one slip that says "reroof the house" or "pave the driveway." Pretty soon all your kids will gladly volunteer for chores.

Don't feel bad about putting your young'uns to work. One of these days they'll have lazy families of their own and will thank you for teaching them how to motivate their kids.

## Passing Out in Front of the Kids

This is downright embarrassing and hard to explain. If you say, "Daddy's asleep," there's always one young'un who'll shoot back, "Why's he sleeping on the picnic table when it's rainin', and why's his false teeth in the grass?"

It's better to just tell them the truth. Once they realize their pa is dead drunk and threw up three hot dogs before passing out, maybe they'll think twice about boozing it up when they get older.

# The Boogeyman:
## Parents' Best Friend

If the fear of a whuppin' won't keep your kids from acting up, you can always fall back on their fear of the boogeyman.

Every little child believes there's a monster hiding under the bed, in the closet, or somewhere just outside the bedroom.

They all imagine it as a big black demon with no real shape— kinda bloblike—and they know it's just waiting for Mama and Daddy to go to sleep so it can EAT ALL THE KIDS IN THE HOUSE!

Tell your young'uns that if they're good, they've got nothing to worry about because good kids taste awful to the boogeyman.

But if they're bad, you'll unlock the bedroom window and help the bad ol' boogeyman come inside.

That might sound cruel to certain folks, but now and then you've got to be mean and nasty parents to help your kids grow up decent. The end justifies the meanness.

When you talk to your young'uns about the boogeyman, be sure to call him exactly that. Don't follow the new "politically correct" trend of calling the monster the "boogeyperson."

If the boogeyman is too terrifying to your brood, you can always tell them he's just make-believe. But quickly warn them that other evil creatures are waiting in the night to snatch them.

# The Haunted Pillow Caper

In Chicken Neck, parents' number-two choice for kid scaring is a weird thing that first showed itself down at the feather pillow factory.

Twenty years ago, the workers there were dumbfounded when pillows suddenly started leaping off the assembly line and bouncing off the walls, as though throwed by an unseen hand.

Some pillow stitchers seated beside the assembly line were hit smack in the face by pillows that busted open and sent up clouds of chicken feathers. The women jumped up and ran screaming out of the building, literally scared sitless.

After a week of these crazy happenings, the factory was knee-deep in chicken feathers. The owner called in Reverend Joshua Boatwright to do an exorcism, and everything returned to normal after the pastor said his piece.

Reverend Boatwright decided the strange events were the work of a poultrygeist.

Ever since then, when local youngsters act up at bedtime, their parents sneak and throw a pillow into the room, then yell, "Better get in bed, kids—the poultrygeist is coming!"

Works every time.

# Give 'Em That Old-Time Religion

To keep your young'uns on the right track, expose them to God early in life.

Drag the whole brood to church at least once a week and make them memorize two or three Bible passages a month. If they don't do it, don't let them watch *Walker, Texas Ranger.*

To emphasize how important it is for your children to attend services, drive them by the local church where there's usually a sign outside that says:

**CH____CH**

**What's Missing?**

Make your kids come up with the correct answer, which is:

**UR**

Which is redneck shorthand for "yoU aRe," and supplies the answer:

**CHURCH**

If your kids get the answer wrong—guessing such things as "couch" or "Chuck Barris"—make 'em sit there in the car until they get it right. Even if it takes hours. Figuring out religious sayings will make a big impact on children.


# Picking the Right Church

Most of our neighbors go to the Baptist or Holiness churches. But as your young'uns get older, let them choose which denomination they want to cozy up to.

Remember, it's not important what kind of church your kids attend. What's important is that they go and go until religion is drilled into their very souls.

You'll know they're religious enough when they start seeing images of our Lord Jesus everywhere—on schoolhouse walls, on cakes of cornbread, and even inside dirty commodes.

We figure all denominations are doing good work as long as they keep your kids from straying down the wrong path.

Why, we wouldn't even object if our children decided to go to a snake-handling church. These are the believers who carry snakes around during services to prove their faith in God. They figure the Lord will keep them from getting bit.

Our oldest boy, Wimpy, used to go to a little country church whose members badly wanted to handle snakes but apparently didn't have enough faith. So they became worm handlers.

These folks let big night crawlers wiggle around in their hands while they shouted at the top of their lungs, "Praise the Lord! Praise Jesus!!"

But four years ago the worm-handling church shut down when somebody stole all their sacred crawlers out of the holy worm box on the altar—interestingly enough, right at the start of bass season.

Even though Sheriff Gardner used be a Green Beret soldier, he never did solve the shocking crime or recover the loot. The sheriff said he figured them church worms had been "baptized with extreme prejudice."

The heartbroke congregation never reopened their church. Most people in town agreed it wasn't no big loss, except maybe during fishing season.

## Give Us This Day Our Daily Cornbread

When we were growing up, we were taught to always kneel beside the bed and say our prayers before going to sleep.

But these days, a lot of kids never get on their knees except when they're shooting dice in the alley or looking under a video game machine for lost quarters.

If you want to raise good kids, teach them to pray properly.

For quite a while, our second oldest son, Beano, prayed for a new bicycle. He didn't get it, and finally one Sunday he asked Reverend Joshua Boatwright why God wasn't answering his prayers.

The pastor just smiled and explained that God is on a different plane.

Beano piped up, "Well, no wonder He didn't hear me— them planes is noisy!"

Although Rufus McKinney insists the One True God is Richard Petty, we believe everybody's got a right to worship the ditty of their choice.

## Skinny-dipping during Baptism

Redneck kids love to swim naked in the river or lake, so naturally they'll beg to do the same when they get baptized. Don't let them do it.

Baptism is a solemn occasion. They ought to at least wear shorts or panties. And don't let 'em take along inner tubes, rubber ducks, or snorkels. The Lord might take offense and burn their naked butts with a lightning bolt!

## Speaking in Unknown Tongues

In some redneck churches, worshipers get gripped by the spirit of Jesus and start shouting in a language nobody understands. This is a phenomenon that can send more chills down your spine than walking barefoot to the outhouse in winter.

We've even seen little bitty kids speak in unknown tongues. We figure anything that keeps children in church and out of trouble is a good thing, so don't discourage your young'uns if they want to try their hand at it.

You never can predict when the "unknown tongues" phenomenon will strike.

One night during services down at the First Church of Our Precious Jesus Christ in His Holy Name, a man jumped out of his seat at the back of the church and started babbling in an unknown tongue. The congregation gathered around him and started shouting and touching him all over, so happy to see somebody moved by the Lord in their midst.

But the man turned out to be a lost Finnish tourist named Olli who was frantically trying to get directions out of town.

## Say Hello to Hell

Every child should be taught about hell.

If one of your young'uns scorches her hand on the stove, smear some salve on it and then turn the experience into a Bible lesson. Tell her she'd better live decent or else she's liable to burn a lot worse in fire and brimstone one of these days.

Chicken Neck's parents have always taught their kids to fear hell. As a result we've got a lot of grown kids so scared of Satan that they won't even buy 6-6-6 fertilizer.

Although nobody knows what hell is really like, we believe it's a lot like Los Angeles—except hell has more movie stars.

## Honky-tonk Survival Skills

When the jukebox starts blaring and the beer starts flowing, a honky-tonk can become one of the most hazardous places on earth. Some decorated war heroes start shaking and crying when told they have to go into a redneck bar.

As your boys and girls get older, don't let 'em set foot near a honky-tonk until they learn the proper ways to act around a crowd of rowdy beer drinkers:

- If a big galoot is in line behind you at the jukebox, turn around and say, "Hey, buddy, what do you want to hear?" You'll save him a quarter and make a friend who just might save your neck when brawls break out later in the evening.

• Always stay alert for flying beer bottles and jars of pig's feet off the bar.

• Keep a close eye on the floor as you walk, or else you'll fall. The combination of sloshed beer and peanut shells is the world's slipperiest stuff. We suspect it's how the ancient Egyptians moved them big pyramid stones across the desert.

• Boys should never say "Hi, there" to any girl whose boyfriend is named "Snake." Especially if he's using a Harley-Davidson sprocket chain for a belt.

You also should be cautious if the boyfriend's got skinny legs. He's sure to be wearing sharp-pointed boots for defense. Some rednecks' metal-tipped boots are so sharp, they cut holes in the floorboards of their pickup trucks.

• Girls should never flirt with any man whose girlfriend is twice her size and has three chins.

Be extra careful if the fat girlfriend appears to be wearing Vanderbilt jeans, but a closer inspection shows the label actually reads Peterbilt.

And quickly move to the other side of the bar if you notice the big-butted gal has a warning device on her rear end that goes "beep, beep, beep" when she backs up.

• When talking to good ol' boys at the bar, mutter "Hell, yeah" and "I heard that" after everything they say.

• Never carry on a conversation unless you've got a toothpick between your teeth or a cigarette dangling out of the side of your mouth. It ain't good manners.

• Never do the three-step in a Texas bar.

• Wear a football mouth guard on Saturday nights, when barroom brawls are more apt to break out. You'll have to sip your beer through a straw, but it's better than buying new teeth.

• If everybody's watching the Nebraska-Florida football game on TV, don't ask the bartender to please turn it to the Princeton-Yale game.

## Entering the Outside World

Rufus McKinney wouldn't live outside of Chicken Neck if you gave him a mansion in Malibu. He likes the simple country life and hates most modern gadgets.

When he finally broke down and bought a VCR to baby-sit his kids, we were downright amazed. But he explained: "I figured it was time to move into the twentieth century."

That's about as far as he moved. Next to the VCR, the newest thing in his house is a fifty-year-old Motorola radio—still tuned to the station that put on *Ted Mack's Original Amateur Hour*.

Every now and then, Rufus flips on the radio to see if ol' Ted is back.

Rufus wouldn't buy a fancy new car even if the Jaguar people held a "buy one, get one free" sale. He's still waiting for Detroit to bring back the Hudson—and swears they're gonna do it, too.

His method of living in the past might sound attractive to some people fed up with the hustle and bustle of the modern world. But let us tell you: America's "good old days" also had plenty of problems, including polio, no air-conditioning, and practically no stock car racing on television.

Sure, they had heroes like John Wayne and Gary Cooper. But we've got Chuck Norris and Alan Autry.

The best way to prepare your kids for entering today's modern society is to let 'em watch plenty of TV.

They'll learn all about the crime, wars, and other problems all over the world—and once they see that, odds are they'll decide to keep their little butts right where they grew up.

# How to Act like a Redneck

Inside every human being there's a little redneck trying to get out. Become an accomplice in the escape by training your kids so they'll be full-fledged rednecks when they grow up:

If you say you're going to do something for somebody, do it. In the redneck nation, a man's word is his bond. We suspect Nike got that Just Do It slogan when one of their salesmen heard it while passing through redneck country.

Southern redneck kids should practice saying "Hell, yeah," "Ah heard that," and "You durn tootin'!" These are basic phrases in the rebel redneck's vocabulary—part of a special ethnic language called "rebonics."

Always refer to the Civil War as "the Wah of North'un Aggression."

Never drive a van unless it's one you use on the job. Van people won't be accepted in redneck society unless they're carpenters, carpet layers, air-conditioning repairmen, and the like.

Van drivers also are required under international redneck rules to keep their van cluttered inside with tools, job materials, RC cans, empty gallon jugs, old fast-food wrappers, and wadded-up cigarette packs. If an inspector stops your van and any of these items are missing, it's a hundred-dollar fine *per item*.

The rear bumper of a pickup truck must have a college football team sticker on it. These can range from UCLA to Nebraska to Tennessee to Texas A & M.

Don't get caught with a Brown or Berkeley sticker on your truck. You'll be stripped naked, driven to the outskirts of town, and told to start walking any direction but south.

**Rednecks keep their tanks FULL during the races**

Plaster your truck with bumper stickers like: I FIGHT POVERTY—I WORK; FIGHT CRIME: SHOOT FIRST; PASS WITH CAUTION: DRIVER CHEWING RED MAN; NO EXCUSES—JUST BUCKLE UP YOUR PANTS; and ASK ME ABOUT MY ILLEGITIMATE CHILDREN.

On the rear window put a radio station sticker—WRED if you can get it—plus NASCAR, NHRA, and National Rifle Association stickers. If your truck's a Ford, add a decal showing Calvin (of Calvin and Hobbes) peeing on a Chevy emblem.

Other rear-window favorites on redneck vehicles: the American flag, Budweiser stickers, and Chuck Norris for President stickers.

If you live in the South, put a rebel flag plate on the front of your truck. We know it ain't politically correct, but rednecks never have given a durn for politics.

When your truck bed rusts and falls off, replace it with a black elastic net. Don't be a cheapo and just stretch a woman's old pair of black net stockings across the bed.

Put a long toolbox in the back of your truck, directly behind the rear window. This has a double purpose: If a relative dies and you're flat broke, you can use the toolbox as a coffin.

---

### Five Ways Rednecks Say "I'm Sorry"

1. "Well, ya know how I am when I git drunk."

2. "Din't know she was yore wife."

3. "Glad it's only a flesh wound."

4. "Here, buddy—have the rest o' my beer."

5. "I'll mow the yard tomorrow, honey."

---

## Beer: It's Not Just for Breakfast Anymore

After Wiley Watkins chopped down six mailboxes while driving to work with a hangover, he stopped washing down his ham and eggs with "the hair of the dog that bit him."

Now Wiley won't touch a beer after midnight, and he ain't had any further accidents. Anybody can benefit from his example.

Warn your grown kids that when they leave the honky-tonk, make sure they're not too drunk to drive. If they're sloshed, tell them to hitch a ride with a sober buddy—or else they could end up buried in a truck toolbox.

## How to Beat Procrastination

Well, we finally got around to writing this chapter.

Most kids would rather put off until tomorrow what they ought to do today, whether it's picking up their clothes or washing the dog. Don't let that happen.

Tell your young'uns they can't leave the house or turn on the TV until they've done what they're supposed to do. And stick to your guns, because this is real important.

We admit that procrastination is a hard habit to break. Our boy Wimpy's been trying to break it for years and still can't get anything done on time.

Annie even went over to the county library and got Wimpy a book on beating procrastination called *Just DO IT, You Lazy Little Twerp*. Now the book is six months overdue and he still ain't read a word.

Uncle Billy's even worse. His procrastination is so bad that he actually applied for a government disability check, claiming he couldn't work because his "problem" kept him from ever showing up for job interviews.

The clerk seriously considered putting him on the disability rolls—probably figuring Billy would never get around to cashing his monthly check anyway.

Don't *you* procrastinate in following our rearin' rules. Start using them today—and you'll wind up the proud parents of the best young'uns in America!